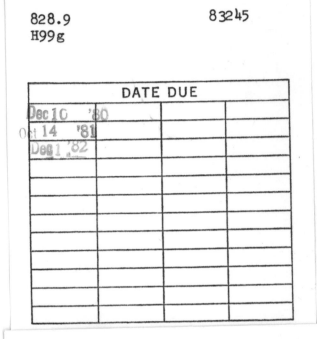

TWENTIETH CENTURY VIEWS

The aim of this series is to present the best in contemporary critical opinion on major authors, providing a twentieth century perspective on their changing status in an era of profound revaluation.

Maynard Mack, *Series Editor*
Yale University

GRAHAM GREENE

A COLLECTION OF CRITICAL ESSAYS

Edited by
Samuel Hynes

Prentice-Hall, Inc.  A SPECTRUM BOOK *Englewood Cliffs, N.J.*

Library of Congress Cataloging in Publication Data

HYNES, SAMUEL LYNN, comp.
    Graham Greene: a collection of critical essays.

    (Twentieth century views) (A Spectrum Book)
    Bibliography: p.
    1. Greene, Graham, 1904–
PR6013.R44Z6335   828'.9'1209   72–8640
ISBN 0–13–362251–7
ISBN 0–13–362244–4 (pbk.)

828.9
H99g
8324s
May 1973

Quotations from Graham Greene's *The Power and the Glory, Brighton Rock,* and *The End of the Affair* are reprinted by permission of The Viking Press, Inc., New York, and Lawrence Pollinger Limited, London.

Acknowledgement is gratefully made to Russel & Volkening, Inc., for permission to reprint from "Germinal," by Æ (copyright 1931 by Diarmuid Russell).

10   9   8   7   6   5   4   3   2   1

PRENTICE-HALL INTERNATIONAL, INC. (*London*)
PRENTICE-HALL OF AUSTRALIA PTY. LTD. (*Sydney*)
PRENTICE-HALL OF CANADA LTD. (*Toronto*)
PRENTICE-HALL OF INDIA PRIVATE LIMITED (*New Delhi*)
PRENTICE-HALL OF JAPAN, INC. (*Tokyo*)

Contents

GRAHAM GREENE

Introduction

by Samuel Hynes

Describing his own work, Graham Greene once remarked that his fixations could best be described as "the melodramatic, the contemporary and later the Catholic novel." Put this way, these terms suggest a development, but in fact all three terms apply to all of Greene's important fiction: neither his methods nor his fixations have changed much. Except for his earliest (of which only *The Man Within* survives), Greene's novels are all set in the contemporary world and often deal with very topical subjects—the Spanish Civil War in *The Confidential Agent,* for example, the Indo-China war in *The Quiet American,* and Duvalier's Haiti in *The Comedians.* Although his novels are perhaps distanced from us by their exotic settings, Greene has nevertheless recorded the world we live in now in terms more wide-ranging and more immediate than those of any other novelist; and if we have an imaginative sense of the violent modern world elsewhere, it is in part because of Greene's writing.

The situations that Greene has chosen for his novels have provided him with the materials of melodrama; his imagination finds its expression in wars and revolutions, and among criminals and police, the hunters and the hunted. These are materials that our world provides in abundance—life in the twentieth century *is* melodramatic, one might reasonably observe—and to say that Greene uses them is simply to say in another way that he writes contemporary novels. But he has not written melodrama for its own sake; he has used it to furnish his world with the texture of violence, terror, and cruelty that he finds in life. And he has used it shrewdly, as a narrative artist, to engage his audience: "If you excite your audience first," he has said, "you can put over what you will of horror, suffering, truth." The excitement must come first—an author must be read—but the end is truth.

For Greene, the truth is religious: not always specifically Catholic, or even Christian in any exact doctrinal sense, but concerned with a vision of human life that postulates the reality of "another world." One could not construct a religion out of Greene's novels, and it seems unlikely that anyone would be converted by reading them, but they are nevertheless the novels of a religious man. Greene has protested that he should be taken as "an author who is a Catholic," rather than as a Catholic author, and in his books, he is obviously an author first—otherwise he would not be read with such pleasure by non-Catholics; but he has also said that every creative writer worth our consideration is "a man given over to an obsession," and Greene's obsession is religious.

The best formulation of that obsession is the quotation from Cardinal Newman that Greene uses as an epigraph to his Mexican travel book, *The Lawless Roads* (U.S. title: *Another Mexico*). It sets the tone, and defines the world of Greene's imagination so well that it is worth quoting in full:

> To consider the world in its length and breadth, its various history, the many races of man, their starts, their fortunes, their mutual alienation, their conflicts; and then their ways, habits, governments, forms of worship; their enterprises, their aimless courses, their random achievements and acquirements, the impotent conclusion of long-standing facts, the tokens, so faint and broken, of a super-intending design, the blind evolution of what turn out to be great powers or truths, the progress of things, as if from unreasoning elements, not towards final causes, the greatness and littleness of man, his far-reaching aims, his short duration, the curtain hung over his futurity, the disappointments of life, the defeat of good, the success of evil, physical pain, mental anguish, the prevalence and intensity of sin, the pervading idolatries, the corruptions, the dreary hopeless irreligion, that condition of the whole race, so fearfully yet exactly described in the Apostle's words, "having no hope, and without God in the world"—all this is a vision to dizzy and appal; and inflicts upon the mind the sense of a profound mystery, which is absolutely beyond human solution.
>
> What shall be said to this heart-piercing, reason-bewildering fact? I can only answer, that either there is no Creator, or this living society of men is in a true sense discarded from His presence . . . *if* there be a God, *since* there is a God, the human race is implicated in some terrible aboriginal calamity.

This is a Victorian priest's view of existence, but it is also contemporary and melodramatic. Newman was describing sinful, fallen man in terms of Christian doctrine, but his vision of humankind—fearful, defeated, and alone—might just as well be described in the contemporary language of alienation and anxiety. And the same is true of Greene's characters; they may be lapsed Catholics, or whiskey priests, but their situations are metaphors for the human condition, and in this fundamental sense Greene's novels are relentlessly contemporary.

They are also contemporary in their political content. Greene himself describes his work as being first political, then Catholic, and then political again, distinguishing early novels such as *It's a Battlefield* and later novels such as *The Quiet American* from the major religious works of his middle period, *Brighton Rock, The Power and the Glory,* and *The Heart of the Matter.* But the separation is not really that clear; Greene's religious views have political implications (Scobie is a political man as well as a religious one), and his politics imply a religious understanding of the human situation. Perhaps, starting from Newman's vision of life, some form of democratic socialism, a system minimizing the power of men to impose suffering on other men, is inevitable.

It is appropriate that a writer of melodramatic, contemporary novels should be the novelist of his generation most clearly influenced by the film, and the first important writer to develop a cinematic technique. Greene's interest in film began early, with the silent films that he saw as a student; during the thirties he wrote scripts, and was a brilliantly severe film critic (Shirley Temple sued him for libel over his review of her *Wee Willie Winkie*), and since then he has continued to write for the films, including adaptations of five of his novels. He is correct to refer to himself, as he does in the *Paris Review* interview, as "a film man."

From films, Greene learned a technique that is at once intimately probing and detached, observing and recording, but allowing the observed circumstances to be their own judgments. Cinematic technique emphasizes the visual context of action, the "world" in which men act out their lives, and Greene is extremely skillful at creating his contemporary scenes out of sharply visualized particulars. Take, for example, the opening paragraph of *The Power and the Glory*:

Mr Tench went out to look for his ether cylinder, into the blazing
Mexican sun and the bleaching dust. A few vultures looked down
from the roof with shabby indifference: he wasn't carrion yet. A
faint feeling of rebellion stirred in Mr Tench's heart, and he
wrenched up a piece of the road with splintering finger-nails and
tossed it feebly towards them. One rose and flapped across the town:
over the tiny plaza, over the bust of an ex-president, ex-general, ex-
human being, over the two stalls which sold mineral water, towards
the river and the sea. It wouldn't find anything there: the sharks
looked after the carrion on that side. Mr Tench went on across the
plaza.

This is almost a shooting script: a long shot of the street; then, pan
to the vultures; in to a closeup of Mr Tench; then, follow the
vulture across the town. It moves as no human eye could, in and
out, viewing the scene with the cold detachment of a camera, a
coldness expressed in the dismissive phrase, "ex-human being."
There are strong feelings in the scene, but they are expressed
primarily through imagery and action—the expressive elements of
the film.[1]

"It is the cinema," says Evelyn Waugh, "which has taught a new
habit of narrative." [2] It is a habit that has not touched all modern
styles (it is not discernible in Waugh's own writing, for example),
but for Greene it has made possible a relation between author and
action that is special and effective. As Waugh remarks, in novels
like Greene's "the writer has become director and producer": that
is, he controls the action, and moves freely about it, but he is not
part of it. His camera eye is like the eye of God, seeing all, but
withholding judgment.

Greene's interest in film is paralleled by his interest in, and use
of, another popular art form, the thriller. Many of his best-known
novels are based on the conventions of the thriller, and several have
been made into successful films. Such involvement with popular
forms may seem to suggest a restricted imagination, or a limited
artistic ambition: in the century of Joyce and Eliot we expect our
serious artists to be drawn to more esoteric models. Greene encourages readers to take a part of his work lightly by calling some
of his novels "entertainments," suggesting that these books do not

[1] See Richard Hoggart's discussion of this point on p. 87.
[2] See below, p. 98.

"carry a message," and have no serious import. But, in fact, there are no real distinctions to be made between novels and entertainments; Greene is always entertaining, and his skillful use of film and thriller conventions explains a good deal of the entertainment, but he is never merely entertaining. He uses popular conventions as elements in a complicated technique that transcends its components and complexly expresses a religious sense of existence.

Greene's place among modern novelists is not with the writers of popular thrillers, therefore, but with the "conscious artists"— with Conrad and James and Ford (all novelists whom he admires). Like those novelists, Greene has an artist's sense of the importance and dignity of his craft; and like them, he has always understood that technique is not enough, that if the novel is to matter, it must be moral.

For Greene, one form of artistic morality is a scrupulous concern for style. Like his contemporary, George Orwell, he sees truth-telling as a primary duty of the artist; Greene explains that in this sense truth is simply *accuracy*—"it is largely a matter of style." The passage that follows this remark is very Orwellian:

> It is my duty to society not to write: "I stood above a bottomless gulf" or "going downstairs, I got into a taxi," because these statements are untrue. My characters must not go white in the face or tremble like leaves, not because these phrases are clichés but because they are untrue. This is not only a matter of the artistic conscience but of the social conscience too. We already see the effect of the popular novel on popular thought. Every time a phrase like one of these passes into the mind uncriticised, it muddies the stream of thought.[3]

This concern for the social consequences of style may seem at variance with Greene's own practice, for his novels, particularly those closest to the thriller conventions, are written in a style that seems intentionally flat and impoverished. But we should remind ourselves that James Joyce, the most self-conscious and artful of modern novelists, aspired to a style of "scrupulous meanness" in *Dubliners*; and that, in modern fiction, art and drabness are not incompatible. Greene's own scrupulously mean style is clearly a

---

[3] Elizabeth Bowen, Graham Greene, V. S. Pritchett, *Why Do I Write?* (London: Percival Marshall, 1948), p. 30.

part of his meaning, an appropriate way of describing the reality
that he sees. For the world that Greene's imagination inhabits is
an impoverished world, diminished by the absence of God, and the
verbal sign of that diminishment is the poverty of his language, the
lack of "aura" in the seen world.

Consider, for example, the style of *A Gun for Sale* (U.S. title:
This Gun for Hire), the best of Greene's "entertainments." A kind of
verbal and imaginative meanness pervades the book; one finds it in
the qualities of imagination of the characters (for instance, in the
vulgar images of Christmas and Christ in Raven's mind), and in the
coarsened, limited imagery and language used to describe the physical setting of the action. Here is a scene in a housing development:

> They had left the little dirty houses behind them. She read the
> name of the new street: Shakespeare Avenue. Bright red bricks
> and Tudor gables and half-timbering, doors with stained glass,
> names like Restholme. These houses represented something worse
> than the meanness of poverty, the meanness of the spirit. They
> were on the very edge of Nottwich now, where the speculative
> builders were running up their hire-purchase houses. It occurred
> to Anne that he had brought her here to kill her in the scarred
> fields behind the housing estate, where the grass had been trampled
> into the clay and the stumps of trees showed where an old wood
> had been.[4]

This is flat writing that reflects the "meanness of spirit" of the
scene. The language is plain and unmetaphorical, the cadences are
broken and unmusical. But it is also vivid writing, exactly descriptive, and more; for out of the description comes a kind of symbolic
resonance. The ordinary world of this episode is a battlefield, as
it often is in Greene, an ugly place, defaced and violated by men;
and the human lives that are lived there are like that scene,
casualties of war.

One can see in such passages how much Greene has charged the
conventions of thriller fiction with significance and judgment. But
the point is that this quality of highly charged drabness, what has
come to be called Greene's "seediness," is a constant aspect of his
style, and that it is a strength, for it gives to his writing that accuracy that he identifies with truth.

[4] *A Gun For Sale* (London: Heinemann, 1936).

In his essay on François Mauriac, Greene laments the loss of the religious sense in the English novel:

> It was as if the world of fiction had lost a dimension: the characters of such distinguished writers as Virginia Woolf and Mr. E. M. Forster wandered like cardboard symbols through a world that was paper-thin. Even in one of the most materialistic of our great novelists—in Trollope—we are aware of another world against which the actions of the characters are thrown into relief. The ungainly clergyman picking his black-booted way through the mud, handling so awkwardly his umbrella, speaking of his miserable income and stumbling through a proposal of marriage, exists in a way that Mrs. Woolf's Mr Ramsay never does, because we are aware that he exists not only to the woman he is addressing but also in a God's eye. His unimportance in the world of the senses is only matched by his enormous importance in another world.[5]

In Greene's novels, the world of the senses is drab and torn by shabby violence, but there is "another world," and because there is, the world that we see has meaning. The other world is removed from men, as God is; but it exists, and the human imagination feeds on it. This is what Greene means when he writes that "creative art seems to remain a function of the religious mind": not that only Christians can write novels, but that great art asserts that life *means,* and that such assertions may be called "religious." And it is in this sense that Greene's melodramatic, contemporary novels are also, as he says, Catholic.

[5] "François Mauriac," *Collected Essays* (London: The Bodley Head, 1969), p. 115.

Graham Greene: The Man Within

Anonymous

Graham Greene writes in his autobiography, *A Sort of Life*:

If I were to choose an epigraph for all the novels I have written, it would be from *Bishop Bloughram's Apology*:

> Our interest's on the dangerous edge of things.
> The honest thief, the tender murderer,
> The superstitious atheist, demi-rep
> That loves and saves her soul in new French books—
> We watch while these in equilibrium keep
> The giddy line midway.

What critic could resist such firm authorial guidance? And especially when the passage does seem to catalogue what is most characteristic in Greene's work—the melodramatic characters and the heightened action on the "dangerous edge," and the precarious moral equilibrium of the actors, between honesty and thievery, between tenderness and murder. As an epigraph, it will certainly do. The trouble is that it points to qualities in the novels which have been too much noticed. Of course Greene has fixed his imagination upon crime and murder, and of course he can tell a story of dangerous action well; but to say so seems to place him among the gifted story-tellers, somewhere near Ambler and Maugham, and obscures his other and more essential affiliation with James and Conrad and Ford, and the great tradition of the novel as a work of art. This seems an appropriate occasion to note that connection, and to assert that in fact Greene is the principal English novelist now writing in that tradition; for did he not invite the connection in 1971 by appearing in a Collected Edition with new introductions by the author (as both James and Conrad did, and Ford wished to do), and by releasing at the same time a memoir of his early years?

Any reader of Greene's *Collected Essays* will have noted another resemblance to James there—the sensitive critic of fiction, interested in technique, almost donnish in his range of literary knowledge, precise and judicious with a careful confidence. Like James, Greene has written best on the novelists of his own tradition: there are several acute essays on James himself, and his appreciations of Ford are simply the best that have been written. And always there is a fine understanding of the craft of fiction, and of the hostility of Englishmen to whatever seems artful; either James or Ford might have written, "It is dangerous in this country to talk about techniques," but in fact Greene did.

The novels show that his interest in technique is not mere talk. One finds in them the same aesthetic tradition in practice: the manipulations of time and point of view, the discreet voice of the primary author, remote but not removed, the dramatically rendered scenes, the impressionistic touches. Remember how the point of view shifts in *The Heart of the Matter*? How the character of Querry is built up by indirections in *A Burnt-Out Case*? The experiment in stream-of-consciousness in *England Made Me*? The topographical use of London in *It's a Battlefield*? In the new introductions to his novels Greene notes some of the technical problems he has faced, and the importance of recognizing them: "How dangerous it is," he writes of *England Made Me,* "for a critic to have no technical awareness of the novel."

Having claimed Greene for the art-novel tradition, one must add at once that he himself has shied away from that connection. In an important essay on Mauriac he acknowledges the greatness of Flaubert and James—"the novel was ceasing to be an aesthetic form and they recalled it to the artistic conscience"—but he assigns to Mauriac a greater role:

> M. Mauriac's first importance to an English reader . . . is that he belongs to the company of the great traditional novelists: he is a writer for whom the visible world has not ceased to exist, whose characters have the solidity and importance of men with souls to save or lose, and a writer who claims the traditional and essential right of a novelist, to comment, to express his views.

When an artist praises another artist in such terms, one may assume that he is describing his own aspirations, and this certainly seems to be true in this case. To Greene, the modern novel has lost the religious sense, "and with the religious sense went the sense of the importance of the human act." Like Mauriac, Greene is concerned to restore that importance and thus to justify the novel in moral as well as in aesthetic terms. This notion is at the centre of his artistic intentions, and for his readers it makes a crucial point: what matters in his novels is not the action, but the moral meaning of the human act—the dangerous edge of things is there.

The right that Greene claims, to comment and to express his views, is one that separates him from the other descendants of James and Conrad. It has made him sometimes didactic, as he admits in his introduction to *Brighton Rock* (which he nevertheless concludes may be the best book he ever wrote); and it has led him to utter the pensées that are perhaps the most distinguishable feature of his style, and to incline toward characters who are themselves penseurs. Greene has made the standard disclaimer of personal responsibility for the remarks of his characters, but in fact his manner is such that it is sometimes difficult to determine the degree of authorial commitment to voiced thoughts. He and his characters think continually about the importance of human acts, about God and the soul, love and damnation, and speak their thoughts in sentences like these: "Point me out the happy man and I will point you out either egotism, evil—or else an absolute ignorance"; "The truth . . . has never been of any real value to any human being—it is a symbol for mathematicians and philosophers to pursue"; "We are all of us resigned to death: it's life we aren't resigned to." These are all from *The Heart of the Matter,* but are they in the voice of Scobie or of Greene? Are they to be regarded as truths, or only as symptoms? This habit of pensée-making is not necessarily a flaw in the novels but it is unsettling to readers and critics unused to the religious sense in fiction.

Greene's didacticism has led to his being identified as a "Catholic novelist," an identification to which he has many times objected. Against this charge he has quoted Newman—"if Literature is to be made a study of human nature, you cannot have a Christian Literature"—but to little avail (a Catholic in support of a Catholic seems a weak defence). Greene might also have called up Auden, who has said that there can no more be Christian art than there can be Christian cookery, and certainly in Auden's sense Greene's novels are not Christian, but are simply the novels of a rather heterodox Christian man. Still, if there is no such thing as Christian literature, there may still be *Catholic* fiction, and in Greene's case it does seem possible to separate the Catholic books from what one might call the lay books. There is no novel by Greene from which the religious sense is entirely absent, but only a few approach sectarianism. One sign of this quality is the way, in certain novels, a priest is given a strong doctrinal speech at the end (this is true of *Brighton Rock, The End of the Affair,* and *The Heart of the Matter,* and, in a rather different way, of *The Power and the Glory*); but this is only one symptom of a more essential peculiarity of those books—the way they all slide off toward abstraction, and away from the felt reality of the visible world, in their final pages. None of these "Catholic" novels ends as well as it began.

Nevertheless it is these novels that have received most of the critical attention that Greene has got. This is no doubt partly because they have offered easy thematic handles and a certain guaranteed seriousness (a novel about damnation *must* be worth writing about), and partly because Catholic critics have rushed in with Catholic explanations; but some of the responsibility is Greene's, for it is he who first distinguished between his "novels" and his "entertainments," and thus encouraged critics to take his best work lightly. His reasons for making the distinction have been various: that the novels were written slowly and the entertainments quickly; that the novels were the products of depressive periods and the entertainments manic; that the entertainments were crime stories, the novels something more. (He has not suggested that the novels are Catholic and the entertainments are lay, though this does seem roughly to be the case.) But none of these explanations validate the distinction, and it is gratifying to see that the new edition calls the whole lot novels. Now, perhaps, Greene's critics will begin to see that *A Gun for Sale* is one of the best and most significant novels of the 1930s, and a far more nearly perfect work of art than *Brighton Rock.*

Greene offers a key to the unity of his fiction in a remark in his introduction to *The Confidential Agent.* He says there that when he began to write that novel he had in mind only "a certain vague ambition to create something legendary out of a contemporary thriller." This seems always to have been Greene's ambition. If a thriller is a novel containing exciting action and crime, then one might say that he has never written anything else; there is violence in all his novels, and crime in most, and one might argue that what makes the theological back-chat of the heaviest novels endurable is the interwoven elements of the thriller—Ali with his throat cut while Scobie thinks about damnation, Pinkie and the vitriol bottle, the knock at the door at the end of *The Power and the Glory*. And even Greene's weakest, dullest novel, *The End of the Affair,* makes miracles tolerable by treating them as unsolved mysteries, almost as crimes.

But the thriller is more than action: it is a set of patterns and conventions as firmly established as those of classical tragedy. Greene mentions some in the introduction quoted above: "the hunted man who becomes in turn the hunter, the peaceful man who turns at bay, the man who has learned to love justice by suffering injustice." These are the materials of his "legends," and as in traditional legends they lend a formality to his violences, and lead us to expect a moral meaning (justice will be done, there will be no open endings, life will be ordered, not sliced). Legend is expressive narrative, and what happens in the narrative happens because it carries meaning; in Greene's novels the violence is not there because the world *is* violent, but because violence satisfies "that moral craving for the just and reasonable expression of human nature left without belief." It is not surprising, then, to find in the novels episodes of violence that are so formal as to be almost allegorical: the killing of Hale, the gas-mask scene in *A Gun for Sale,* the two deaths of Harry Lime, the murder of Else in *The Confidential Agent.* In this imagined world the action that matters is the eternal spiritual war between good and evil, and the novels are the legends of the battlefield.

The legendary quality of Greene's writing has to some extent been obscured by the particularity of his imagined world. His settings have been so consistently vivid and actual that they have been given a collective name—"Greeneland"—and a descriptive adjective—"seedy." Greene objects to both the noun and the adjective, but he can scarcely deny that his world *is* consistently seedy, sordid, violent and cruel. These qualities are part of the legend:

they describe not an actual environment, but an image of a spiritual condition—a world abandoned by God. Greene is a man with a commitment to a religious tradition which he cannot see as manifested in contemporary society: there is no apparent way of expressing belief with *these* physical, human materials—one can only express the absence of belief. Perhaps the best expression of this sense of the world is in the long passage from Newman which stands as an epigraph to *The Lawless Roads*. In it Newman describes the fearful, suffering condition of men, and concludes:

> What shall be said to this heart-piercing, reason-bewildering fact? I can only answer, that either there is no Creator, or this living society of men is in a true sense discarded from His presence . . . *if* there be a God, *since* there is a God, the human race is implicated in some terrible aboriginal calamity.

One might say that in Greene's novels that calamity goes on, a continuing evidence that men have been discarded from God's sight. Hence not only the "seedy" texture of the novels, and the insistent violence, but also the tone of horror and disgust, a tone which sometimes seems to be in excess of the circumstances: for the most important fact about Greene's world is that God has abandoned it, and that fact cannot be represented as a part of the world, but only as an emotion about it. There is, therefore, a correlation between the banality and ugliness of this world and the spiritual emptiness of it, and this correlation is most powerful and emotionally affective when it appears simply as legend—that is in the "entertainments."

Greene might perhaps protest that this view of his novels assumes them to be all of a piece, and makes no allowance for differences among them, or for development. One might of course divide the novels into categories—the English novels and the Tropical or Equatorial novels—or into periods—the prewar novels and the postwar novels; and one might note in the later work a creeping benevolence, rising to the comical résumé of his entire career, revisited in the company of his Muse, a raffish old Catholic lady, in *Travels with my Aunt*. But Greene remains a novelist in whom the changes are minor, and the unity overwhelming; the locales of his novels may change, but the imagination has remained a constant from the beginning.

Greene's own theories of the shaping of his mind confirm this reading of his work, for he has always stressed the formative influences of early experience, and the continuity of consciousness. One form of this theory is what Greene calls the "Judas Complex" —the idea that the cruelties and betrayals of adult lives are born in childhood, that guilts are rooted in innocence. The theory appears in Greene's autobiographical essay, "The Lost Childhood," where it is epitomized in a quotation from a poem by A. E.:

> In the lost boyhood of Judas
> Christ was betrayed.

The same theme (with the same quotation) also appears in the story "The Basement Room," and in a less sombre form it is a principal thesis of *A Sort of Life,* which begins: "If I had known it, the whole future must have lain all the time along those Berkhamsted streets."

A curious sub-heading of this theory of childhood is Greene's insistence on the importance of one's early reading. "Perhaps it is only in childhood that books have any deep influence on our lives," he writes in "The Lost Childhood," and *A Sort of Life* repeats the thought: "The influence of early books is profound." Greene has always been fond of returning to those early books—to Rider Haggard and Anthony Hope and Marjorie Bowen—and has repeatedly testified to their influence on his own work. "One's life is more formed, I sometimes think, by books than by human beings," he has his character Pulling think in *Travels with my Aunt*: "it is out of books one learns about love and pain at second hand."

Greene seems to find comfort in the thought that life is all embryonically there in childhood, and that the images found innocently and accidentally in one's first reading become the defining images of one's vision of experience. As a theory of human psychology this seems very dubious, but as a theory of Greene's own imagination it is revealing. When he says in his essay on the young Dickens that "the creative writer perceives his world once and for all in childhood and adolescence," Greene is making at most a generalization about his *kind* of writer, and identifying the psychic sources of his own legends, of the hunted man and the peaceful man and the man who has suffered injustice; like Dickens, he has found the images of childhood fears that are never outgrown.

The implications of this theory for Greene's novels are considerable. For one thing, the theory implies a rather special view of character—that it is our origins, and not events, that shape us. "How little in truth are we changed by events," he writes; "how romantic and false . . . is a book such as Conrad's *Lord Jim*." His characters have hearts, not histories (how hollow the psychological explanation of Pinkie's evil rings), and the significant changes in his novels are changes of heart. Events can only kill or cure, they cannot save. Plot, therefore, is at best a conventional legendary frame; as Querry says: "The subject of a novel is not the plot. Who remembers what happened to Lucien de Rubempré in the end?" If neither character nor plot matters, then what does? One is tempted to reply, *souls* do, the shapes and meanings of the religious sense do, changes of heart do, though such a reply seems to return Greene to the simplifications of his co-religionists.

It is consistent with Greene's theory of the imagination that his autobiography should break off in 1932, with the publication of his first success, *Stamboul Train*. For by then the writer had been formed, and the images stored: there was nothing left but the living and the writing. *A Sort of Life* has the virtue of good autobiography: it is frank, honest, and entertaining. As an account of a Georgian boyhood and youth it has value quite apart from the importance of its subject—though one must add that it seems a bit heavier on fear and weakness than your ordinary Georgian boyhood. As a personal record, it adds little that is surprising to what Greene has already written about himself, but it does make his early life rather less melodramatic, by filling in the spaces between the suicide attempts and the Russian roulette. It provides some particular sources for fictional episodes, and it reinforces Greene's theories about the relations between art and life—that is to say between *his* art and *his* life.

Another kind of autobiography emerges from the introductions to the new Collected Edition: the life of Greene-the-Adventurer and Greene-the-Professional, travelling to Sierra Leone, Cuba, and Tabasco, writing his novels, and sometimes judging them. It is interesting to note, after all these years in which Greene has fought against the influence of Conrad, that his introductions are very like Conrad's, and not at all like James's; they are personal and anecdotal, and focus on the occasions of the novels rather than on the creating mind. It is an engrossing story, but the introductions are minor and supplementary, far less important to an understanding of Greene than a few of his essays are.

But most of all, the Collected Edition is important as a monument to a major English novelist's achievement. Greene has done what he aimed to do—he has expressed a religious sense, and created a fictive world in which human acts are important. In that world, at least, creative art is a function of the religious mind; Greene would have it that this is always so. His art is perhaps little comfort to the religious, for it offers no confirmation of comfortable words, and if it celebrates, it celebrates minimal virtues. But art has other things to do besides comforting and celebrating; it can feed our imaginative lives by insisting that the religious sense exists, in this world, in Brighton and Tabasco and Indo-China. No one has done that better in fiction than Graham Greene.

Graham Greene: The Earlier Novels

by Derek Traversi

The writings of Graham Greene raise to a very high degree the general problem of the place in art of elements of experience which correspond to some thwarting of ordinary impulses, which we might call, in the widest sense of the word, "abnormal." It is clear that "abnormality" of this kind has been compatible with the highest degree of creative achievement; Dostoievsky is an obvious case in point, and there are many others. Common, however, to all the great writers of so-called "abnormal" tendencies is the discovery, through their particular form of expression, of a means to transcend mere eccentricity and to give their experience a universal validity. In many cases—and here again Dostoievsky is an example—religion has served as a kind of objective counter to what might otherwise have been, and indeed often were, personal extravagances. Religion, in other words, has been in such cases a normalizing, universalizing element in the creative process. This, however, does not always or necessarily occur. Far from objectivizing their emotion by reference to an external standard (religious or otherwise), writers of the type we are considering frequently turn in upon themselves, use their art as a means of dwelling upon the eccentric elements in their make-up, exacerbate themselves in a kind of emotional acceptance of sheer frustration. In such cases the presence of avowed religious interests affords only a partial key to the true nature of an inspiration which derives, at least to some extent, from experiences of a different kind. It is to this type of creative activity, in which the presence of a coherent spiritual conception is desired, *willed* as an end without being fully accepted or assimilated, that the novels of Graham Greene belong.

The characteristic qualities of Graham Greene's inspiration are best approached through a consideration of the peculiar obliquity which, more especially in his earlier novels, he imparts to his writing. The following passages, both taken from *England Made Me,* are representative:

> Many things there are to consider over thirty years, things seen and heard and lied about and loved, things one has feared and admired and felt desire for, things abandoned with the sea gently lifting and the lightship dropping behind like a small station on the Underground, bright at night and empty, no one getting out and the train not stopping.
>
> He didn't like girls, he couldn't have said it in words more plainly; tawdry little creatures, other people's sisters, their hats blocking the view at Lords'.

Both these passages are concerned with the relationship between past memories and present feeling; and both leave us, in their different ways, with an impression of incoherence and lack of unity. The past overshadows the present without dominating it; the present, constantly aware of the past, strives in vain to assimilate it. The catalogue which comprises the earlier part of the first passage, although it clearly reflects a mood of mingled weariness and nostalgia, evades the real definition of emotion by surrender to an effect in which rhythm is more important than precision. The "things abandoned," "seen and heard and lied about and loved," are left in obscurity, and the lightship and the Underground station lend no more than a marginal touch of concreteness to what are essentially broken emotions groping uncertainly towards definition. The second passage shows even more clearly the difficulty which all Greene's characters experience in relating their emotional reactions to a definite cause. The only reason indicated for the unexpressed but pervasive resentment against "girls" which the passage conveys —and which is a constant and recurrent theme in all Greene's work —is the indirect reference to a childhood impression obviously disproportionate to its supposed effects. The psychological hint, in short, covers inadequately what is once more a failure in artistic communication. The impression conveyed by both passages is finally the same. The subconscious memories of Anthony Farrant and Minty's schoolboy reactions are clearly present, deeply embedded, somewhere in their mature experience; but in both cases the projection of these memories suggests an emotional situation which has failed to attain full self-consciousness. Both reflect the author's tendency to tail off, at the moment of definition, into the frustrated and the desultory, a tendency which all his characters share and which he strives in all his work to overcome.

That the elements which determine this frustration are intimately connected with childhood experience can be detected in Greene's first writings. At the back even of his early short stories is a rooted incapacity to come to terms with his environment, and more especially with the implications of his own maturity. The child in *The End of the Party* (1929), obsessed by a fear of darkness which he relates half-consciously to the terror of death, moves already in a world with which Greene's mature protagonists are familiar. Driven by his own deeply-ingrained fear of confessing weakness to go to the very children's party, which he associates through previous experience with a terror as sinister as it is undefinable, he finally dies, during the game of "hide-and-seek," in the dark which he has been expecting with fascinated horror throughout the day. He is, in other words, the victim of a chase in which his own repressed fears serve as instruments of persecution. These fears are intensified by his attitude to the adult world, and in particular to his parents. The boy Francis is torn between the desire to relieve his own fears by expressing them ("He could almost hear himself saying those final words, breaking down for ever, as he knew instinctively, the barrier of ignorance that saved his mind from his parents' knowledge") and the horror of meeting, instead of comprehension, "the expression of amazement in his mother's face, and then the cold confidence of a grown-up's retort." Attention to the phrasing here reveals that some, at least, of the true motives of the emotional conflict do not lie on the surface. The confession to which the child cannot bring himself is impeded by a sense of shame which is clearly in excess of the given facts. It would involve, we are told, the breaking-down "for ever" of the "barrier of ignorance that *saved* his mind from his parents' knowledge"; confession would bring with it a change in the child's relation to his parents that would last "for ever," would put an end to the state of ignorance which is felt obscurely to have a "saving" quality, to provide protection against what would prove, once brought into the open, an unspeakable catastrophe.

The precise nature of this catastrophe escapes definition; indeed, it could almost be said that to define it is the underlying purpose of all Greene's work. Evidently it involves a distortion of ordinary sentiment which, while it may have its roots in childhood experiences, concerns the mature personality of the author. This is already implied in the description quoted of the child's state of mind when he faces the possibility of confession. The phrase "as he knew instinctively" tells us that what we are reading is not a direct re-creation of childhood (in so far as that is possible) but an explanation in terms of adult vision of what goes on in a child's mind. The difference illuminates considerably the nature of the feelings with which the author is here concerned. They are clearly related to the persistent resentment against sex which figures so prominently in everything that Graham Greene has written. The child, indeed, is made to relate this resentment to his own consuming fear: "His cheeks still bore the badge of *a shameful memory,* of the game of hide-and-seek last year in the darkened house, and of how he screamed when Mabel Warren put her hand suddenly on his arm." And again: "Their long pigtails swung superciliously to a masculine stride. *Their sex humiliated him,* as they watched him fumble with his egg, from under lowered scornful eyelids." It is this sense of humiliation, associated with adolescent impressions of sex, that prompts the child's resistance to confessing the fear which is one of its manifestations, and so contributes to the creation of his impression of an exterior universe which runs counter to the intimate necessities of his being, and drives him to disaster. "God"—to whom the boy prayed, in confidence that his ordeal would somehow be avoided—"had done nothing for him, and the minutes flew." Tragedy, in Greene's most characteristic work, is associated with an inner conviction of betrayal.

In *England Made Me* (1935), the most ambitious of the early novels, preoccupations of the same kind are related to a wider pattern of experience. Once more the instrument of tragedy is the lack of correspondence between the inner and the outer man; and protagonists, in their efforts to attain a satisfactory way of living, are foiled not by external circumstances, but by prejudices, whose effects reach forward from childhood origins into adult life, and so prevent them from accepting fully the environment in which they live. The central theme of the novel is the relationship, at once inescapable and elusive, between a brother and a sister. Anthony and Kate Farrant are bound together by memories of a common education, to which, however, they have reacted in contrasted ways; and in their reaction the author has sought to polarize two worlds, two conceptions of society, whose simultaneous existence is a reflection of the state of contemporary man. Cosmopolitan Stockholm and suburban London represent two worlds, between which the protagonists are torn, and in neither of which they can find a spiritual home. Bound, on the one hand, by traditions which have degenerated into mere prejudices and conscious, on the other, of a freedom which is sterile because, deprived of spiritual foundations, brother and sister are involved logically in a tragedy which reflects the mixture of attraction and repulsion towards the family bond, that is the decisive element in their natures.

The consequences of this bond are apparent in their character. Anthony remains attached to the sentiments and prejudices of English suburban society as instilled into him by a painful and insensitive process of education. Once more we are aware of Greene's preoccupation with the formative (or deforming) influences at work upon adolescence. "The beating in the nursery, the tears before the boarding school . . . the beating in the study when he brought home the smutty book with the pretty pictures"; these are memories which, although Anthony's later life is clearly a reaction against them, are still full of meaning for him. "Honour," "love," "the family," are words which still evoke in him a response, although it is also a repudiation of all they stand for that he has degenerated into an adventurer whose sentiments, long since turned as shabby as his dress, are no longer able to rule his life, but only to prevent him from achieving success in a ruthless and impersonal world. Kate, on the other hand, has, at the expense of normal human feeling, broken through the tyranny of her own past. She has long since cut, by the violent exercise of her stronger will, the more superficial bonds that connect her with her family and education. Determined to exclude from her life anything that might prejudice her own interests, she has become, by the sheer confidence with which she has handled her sexual assets, the mistress of the great international financier Krogh, and has accepted the new world of sterile selfishness in which attachments, whether to family, class, country, or belief, have no place. And yet, contrasted as they are, the two are bound together by bonds of affinity, which prevent either from accepting fully the way of life they have chosen. Kate, thinking of Anthony and looking back over her own path to success, confesses the importance of the despised sentimental motives in forming her decisions. She concludes that she "plotted for this, planned for this, that we should be together again"; Anthony, recalled to her side after long separation, assumes instinctively the position of her guide and protector and so deprives himself of the very fruits of success to which, as an adventurer, his efforts had been directed.

More interesting than the fact of this relationship, however, for the light it throws upon the author's inspiration, is its peculiar nature. Behind the bond that unites brother and sister Graham Greene characteristically places the indelible memory of a particular moment in childhood; the moment when the boy Anthony, having broken through the fear that haunts him in the company of his school-fellows, meets his sister secretly in a barn, and is sent back by her to the first steps in a life of shabby rebellion against ingrained conformity. To this moment, indeed, Anthony ascribes the origins of what amounts to a spiritual deformity. The man's character, in short, is shaped by the boy's resentment against a decision imposed on him by his sister's greater strength of will. Kate herself realizes the harm she has done and devotes herself, with all the family feeling that remains latent behind her assumed self-sufficiency, to make amends for it. It is her desire to undo "the *damage* I did when I sent him back, back from the barn to conform, to pick up the conventions, the manners of all the rest" that inspires her to use her power to discover "a way out" for him in Krogh's employment; just as it is his own subjection to the "conventions" that prevents him, in the long run, either from following his own instinct to "break away" or from accepting the solution she has proposed for him. The author clearly intends that the catastrophe which overtakes brother and sister alike should be held to follow logically from this original flaw in their relationship.

It is characteristic of Greene that the triviality of this incident, or at least of the external facts upon which it is based, is out of all proportion to the seriousness of its effects. A sense of regret felt by

two adults for an acute childhood memory of liberation—"for the
Bedford Palace, the apples they'd eaten to take the smell away"—
clearly cannot sustain the burden of deeper significance placed
upon it. There is little doubt that behind the relationship between
Anthony and Kate, behind the crucial moment in the barn, there
lie once more—as in *The End of the Party*—motives to which the
author himself is unable to give clear definition. Of these motives
Kate is at moments dimly conscious: "His was the weakness that
should have been hers, the uncertainty, the vanity, the charm of
something rash and unpremeditated. *It was the nearest she could
get to completeness,* having him here and in the same room." The
emotional implications of this "completeness" are evidently more
complex than the symbolic scheme of the novel would lead one to
suppose. They are most clearly expressed when Kate announces her
intention to marry Krogh. The tangled web of motives which
emerges as a result of this announcement is very close to the ambiguous core of the novel. Kate, in marrying Erik Krogh, looks
beyond the husband she has chosen to the more intimate bond
that unites her to her brother. She is moved largely by the thought
that she will be able to extract from the financier a settlement for
Anthony; we are told that she "might have been marrying Anthony
and not Erik at all," and her immediate reaction is to bring the
news to her brother. Anthony's opinion is in turn characteristically
double, involving both the adventurer and the devoted brother.
"Incorrigibly conventional," "hopelessly innocent," he appeals to
the set of feelings to which he still gives the name of "love" and
protests against the proposed marriage: "You can't. . . . You don't
love him"; at the same time he sees in his freshly acquired knowledge of Krogh's financial weakness and illegal manœuvres a unique
opportunity for blackmail. Most ambiguous of all, however, and
most closely related to the emotional impulse behind the novel, is
Kate's attitude to her brother at this decisive moment. The full
meaning of her retort to his protest—"I love you"—only emerges
from the obscurity of the whole episode, if at all, as a result of
Anthony's continued embarrassment.

> "That's not the point." He was worried; he was muddled; he said
> something under his breath about "children" and blushed with self-
> consciousness.
>
> Kate said: "I'm sterile. You needn't be afraid," and seeing his

embarrassment, added *with an enraged despair:* "I don't want them.
I've never wanted them," and felt her body stretch to receive him.

Here, if anywhere, the author's ostensible purpose is related to the
personal issues which dominate the lives of his characters. Although
Kate's sterility is that of the world which she has deliberately
chosen as her own, the motives of her choice are fundamentally,
if obscurely, personal. If that sterility is reflected everywhere in
Krogh's impersonal constructions of glass and steel, in the whole
spirit of his organization, it yet corresponds to the nature which
impelled Kate to ally her own fate with that of the great industrial-
ist. Her sterility, in short, is bound up with her attitude to the past
supremely represented in her brother, towards whom her body
stretches in an impossible, and therefore sterile, desire. Throughout this passage, and others in which Greene seems to be struggling
with half-revealed feelings in his effort to give substance to the
relationship between the Farrants, we are aware that emotion is
not adequately projected, that the internal necessity and the external situation are not satisfactorily related. The persistence of
this obscurity is the sign of failure in communication which the
author, in his later work, seeks to overcome by the introduction of
religious values.

The religious motive, which plays an increasing part in all
Greene's later work, makes a faint, hesitating appearance in *England Made Me.* It suffers, significantly, from being itself founded
on the very intimate frustrations which it aims at overcoming. Most
of Greene's "religious" characters, of whom Minty is a preliminary
sketch, represent an impossible effort to build something positive
out of embitterment and frustration. Minty's emotions are founded
on the usual adolescent memories, with their characteristic associa-
tions of repression and perversion: " 'I see you were at the old
place,' he said. 'Those were the days, eh? . . . I don't suppose
you'd remember old Tester (six months for indecent assault)' " Resentment against the herd, and beneath it a rooted sense of sexual
inferiority, turns easily into the resentment against life which
Greene's characters are inclined to substitute for positive religious
values and which finds expression in the hatred of the normal
human activities from which they feel themselves excluded. The
accidental cause and the permanent resentment are typically associated in many of Minty's reflections:

The body's shape, the running nose, excrement, the stupid postures
of passion, these beat like a bird's heart in Minty's brain. . . . A
gang of schoolboys raced through Minty's mind, breaking up his
pictures of Madonna and Child, jeering, belching, breaking wind.

That emotions of this kind have any necessary connection with
religious belief is open to question. Beyond the intense feeling generated by personal resentment, religion is only present as a kind of
mechanical superstition, involving the appeasement of forces im-
perfectly discerned but associated with the relentless persecution of
the individual by the herd. Life—so Greene's characters seem continually tempted to argue—hunts down the isolated victim, worms
out of him his most shameful and closely guarded secrets, visits
upon him, through his own baffled and inferior emotions, the consequences of his own intimate weakness; and, once "life" has been
in some obscure way equated with the operations of destiny, the
only possible defence is a gesture of propitiation, the adherence
to a rite which is itself imposed upon the individual as something
incomprehensible and alien. Upon his capacity to make of religion
something more than a projection of accidental and eccentric personal qualities will depend any definite estimate of Graham
Greene's permanent value as an artist.

Brighton Rock (1938) represents Greene's first real attempt to
relate his peculiar preoccupations to a more ample framework of
beliefs. Ostensibly a study of adolescent criminality it involves an
elaborate effort to demonstrate the workings of providential justice
through the logical implications of crime. The surrender to criminal impulses is the beginning of a long chain of transgressions;
having murdered Hale to counter the fear of betrayal, the adolescent Pinkie is driven, in order to preserve his secret, first to murder
a second companion, Spicer, and then to marry the innocent
waitress, Rose, who knows (or so he fears) his secret and who may
otherwise be obliged, by giving evidence, to betray him. The conception fits admirably the author's tendency to *hunt* his characters,
to see them as surrounded by a society which closes remorselessly in
upon them and, by the very exploitation of their own fears and
shame, eventually destroys them. In this case, however, the victim
is a criminal and the persecution, although ostensibly the work of
man, is in the hands of God. The avenging instrument is Ida
Arnold, the promiscuous, friendly, accommodating woman who

pursues the murderer with an intense conviction that derives from her acceptance of the ordinary values of society; "I know," she says repeatedly, "the difference between Right and Wrong." What she really knows, it is suggested, is the meaning given to these terms by the world in which she lives:

> Someone had made Fred unhappy, and somebody was going to be made unhappy in turn. An eye for an eye. If you believed in God, you might leave vengeance to him, but you couldn't trust the One, the universal spirit. Vengeance was Ida's, just as much as reward was Ida's, the soft gluey mouth affixed in taxis, the warm handclasp in cinemas, the only reward there was. And vengeance and reward— they were both fun.

Once more we are aware of the author's desire simultaneously to join in the hunt and to feel for the victim. Ida Arnold is at once the instrument of justice and a caricature of the conventional conception of morality: her stature as a moral instrument is diminished by the sneer implied in the reference to "the One, the universal spirit" and by the tone, in which repulsion and attraction are oddly mingled, of "the soft gluey mouth affixed in taxis, the warm handclasp in cinemas." The conflict of values here is rather a projection of intimate obscurity than an expression of true complexity. There is no real reason, apart from a personal resentment against accepted standards whose roots are purely accidental, why these standards should be caricatured by association with the physical presence of Ida; and it is at least arguable that, as the interpretation of popular psychology which it sets out to be, the whole passage is an unreal expression of thwarted prejudice.

The existence of a contrast between the values of society and the twisted moral preoccupations imposed upon the hero should not blind us to the connection that exists between them. If Pinkie is hunted to an end that we know from the first to be a foregone conclusion, the means by which society, through Ida, brings him to his doom lie in his own thwarted, contradictory impulses. Pinkie's criminality, indeed, is an instinctive reaction against the pressure, the obligation to conform, which is Greene's constant obsession. Once more the roots of rebellion lie in a barely definable childhood experience of desertion. The isolation of the schoolboy in the asphalt playground, when "the cracked bell clanged and the children came towards him with a purpose"; the more intimate loathing of sexual experience, traced back to the child's memories of "the frightening weekly exercise of his parents" watched "from his single bed" with a terrifying sense of exclusion, from something at once mysterious and revolting: such are the foundations of Pinkie's spiritual outlook. His criminality is the product of a characteristic combination of innocence and experience. He has never touched intoxicating liquor, "never yet kissed a girl"; the razor is for him an instinctive means of defence against a society from whose normal emotions he feels himself excluded but which will, in the end, use the very abnormality it has fostered in him to hunt him down to destruction.

In this process the decisive part is played by the strongest of all his twisted emotions—the reaction against normal sexuality which emerges so powerfully in his attitude to the girl he has unwillingly married. The Boy is, from the sexual point of view, a rare combination of knowledge and innocence. Though we are told that "he knew everything," though "he had watched every detail of the act of sex" so that "you couldn't deceive him with lovely words, there was nothing to be excited about, no gain to recompense you for what you lost," the impulse which really moves him and explains his premature disillusionment is one of resentment for having inexplicably missed something which he cannot himself define. His resentment against sex is, in fact, itself based on sexual craving, and only in sexual terms can it be defined. "His virginity"—we are told—*"straightened in him like sex"*; and—on another occasion—"he watched Rose *with his soured virginity,* as one might watch a draught of medicine offered that one would never, never take—one would die first—or let others die." It is this attitude which, translated into action, launches Pinkie upon the anti-social career which eventually leads him to destruction. The defiance of society which finds expression in the ruthlessness, the razor-slashing, the search for security through murder are all, in the last analysis, manifestations of this intimate, barely definable sexual resentment.

This resentment is closely bound up, in turn, with the execution of justice. Hating the very thought of sexual contact, the Boy is driven, to ensure his own safety, to marry the faded, inexperienced Rose, to whom chance, or the operations of a mysterious providence, has given the possibility of denouncing him. He marries her

in a shabby registry office, only to find that circumstances have imposed, upon what seemed to be an act of momentary convenience,
consequences that are permanent and inescapable: "they couldn't
make a wife give evidence, but nothing could prevent a wife
except love." It is at this point that Catholicism which corresponds,
as an intimate instrument of vengeance, to the external persecution
of society, makes its appearance. Pinkie and Rose are both Catholics; and both are, as Catholics, excluded by the possession of certain *knowledge* from the ignorance that might have saved them.
Both in particular are convinced of the eternal consequences of
their temporal acts. To Ida Arnold's instinctive acceptance of the
social standards of moral behaviour—"I know the difference between Right and Wrong"—standards essentially instinctive, superficial, they oppose a conviction that the more profound distinction
is one, imposed upon the conscience and objectively defined, between Good and Evil. In contracting marriage, both Pinkie and
Rose are fully aware of their responsibility. "What was the good
of praying now?"—Rose asks herself, the morning after her marriage—"She'd finished with all that; she had chosen her side; if they
damned him they'd got to damn her too." And again, a little later:
"she knew by tests as clear as mathematics that Pinkie was evil."

"She knew by tests as clear as mathematics." It is here, surely,
that the peculiar nature of Greene's Catholicism makes itself felt
in what is, after all, a begging of the fundamental questions. The
author makes his dramatic effect by simplifying the moral issues
with which he is dealing. At the same time as he insists on the
ease with which the distinction between good and evil can be
grasped by applying simple religious tests his whole novel seems
devoted to proving that, in point of fact, his characters are not
fully responsible, not in a position fully to understand what they
are doing. He seems, in effect, to plead simultaneously for their
own peculiar "abnormality" and for the framework of beliefs which
is superficially imposed upon them. The two attitudes simply do
not unite. The Boy's disgust at the "frightening weekly exercise"
on the bed has not, essentially, any relation to the theological doctrine of Original Sin. It is something far more limited, irrational
and even selfish; it is, indeed, no more than the development of a
small child's resentment in the presence of something which he
does not understand and from which he feels himself excluded:

"He was filled with hatred, disgust, loneliness: he was completely abandoned: he had no share in their thoughts—for the space of a few minutes he was dead, he was like a soul in purgatory watching the shameless act of a beloved person." The Catholicism which derives from such feelings, far from pointing to personal stability, can only be—as it is in this case—an additional pretext for maintaining the moral ambiguity upon which the author's inspiration depends.

In the light of the resentment upon which it is founded *Brighton Rock* appears as the projection of an obscure relationship between personal inhibitions and an objective structure of belief which has no necessary connection with them. The effort to straighten out a profound emotional twist certainly exists in the novel. There is an indication of this at the end when Pinkie, engaged in driving Rose to suicide so that he may be rid of the eternal burden with which he has loaded himself, confessed that not all in their relationship has been loathing and hatred: "He hadn't hated her; he hadn't even hated the act. There had been a kind of pleasure, a kind of pride, a kind of—something else." But this recognition, upon which a fuller, more human emotion might have been based, to serve as the foundation for a truly adult moral conception, is resisted, fails to prosper. The forces of adolescent resentment return with double force to impose the tragedy for which, at bottom, they crave. "He withstood it, with all the bitter force of the school bench, the cement playground, the St Pancras waiting-room, Dallow's and Judy's secret lust, and the cold unhappy moment on the pier." There is no doubt that it is in this resistance, rather than in the abstract framework of moral certainties, that the author's own emotions are most deeply involved. The frustrated bitterness which is his inheritance and his problem takes control of Pinkie once more, drives him to be again, as throughout the book, the instrument of his creator's impossible attempt to found an acceptance of objective moral doctrines upon the accidents of a thwarted personal experience. *Brighton Rock* leaves us with a sense that, in comparison with the real urgency of a personal problem that evades expression, the theological framework of the novel is founded upon ambiguity and is therefore, in the last analysis, unreal.

The Best and the Worst

by Morton Dauwen Zabel

I

"There was something about a fête which drew Arthur Rowe irresistibly, bound him a helpless victim to the distant blare of a band . . . called him like innocence: it was entangled in childhood, with vicarage gardens, and girls in white summer frocks, and the smell of herbaceous borders, and security." We meet him—in one of those opening pages we have come to recognize as seizing the attention with the immediate spell of the born conjuror—in the blitzed and gutted London of the early 1940s, stumbling on a charity bazaar in a Bloomsbury square: a man alone and a murderer but fearless because he has made a friend of his guilt. When he gave his wife the poison that released her from the suffering he pitied he had not asked her consent; "he could never tell whether she might not have preferred any sort of life to death." A fortune-teller slips him, mistakenly, the password by which he wins a cake in the raffle. But there are others who want it and the thing concealed in its heart. Visited that night in his shabby room by a cripple, Rowe has barely tasted the hyoscine in his tea when out of a droning sky a bomb drops, explodes the house, and blows him and us into a dream of horrors—man-hunt, spies, sabotage, amnesia, murders, and suicide: an "entertainment" by Graham Greene.

Again we enter the familiar spectre of our age—years of fear and mounting premonition in the 1930s, war and its disasters in the forties, its aftermath of treachery and anarchy still around us

"The Best and the Worst." From *Craft and Character*, by Morton Dauwen Zabel (New York, N.Y.: The Viking Press, Inc., 1957), pp. 76–96. Copyright © 1943 and 1956 by Morton Dauwen Zabel. Reprinted by permission of The Viking Press, Inc.

in the fifties: no matter what the decade, Greene's evocation of it through fourteen novels (of which *The Ministry of Fear* may be taken as typical of those he calls "entertainments") invariably brings with it an effect that he has made classic of its time and that has justly won him the title "the Auden of the modern thriller." Here once more is the haunted England of the Twentieth Century, the European nightmare of corruption and doom, a *Blick ins Chaos* where

> taut with apprehensive dreads
> The sleepless guests of Europe lay
> Wishing the centuries away,
> And the low mutter of their vows
> Went echoing through her haunted house,
> As on the verge of happening
> There crouched the presence of The Thing.
> All formulas were tried to still
> The scratching on the window-sill,
> All bolts of custom made secure
> Against the pressure on the door,
> But up the staircase of events
> Carrying his special instruments,
> To every bedside all the same
> The dreadful figure swiftly came.[1]

The fustian stage-sets of Oppenheim, Bram Stoker, and Edgar Wallace are gone with their earlier innocent day. We are in a world whose fabulous realities have materialized appallingly out of contemporary legend and prophecy—the portentous journalism of Tabouis, Sheean, Thompson, Gunther, and the apotheosis of the foreign correspondent; the films of Lang, Murnau, Renoir, and Hitchcock; the Gothic fables of Ambler, Hammett, and Simenon; the putsches, pogroms, marches, and mobilizations that have mounted to catastrophe in the present moment of our lives. Its synthetic thrills and anarchic savagery are ruses of melodrama no longer. Guilt pervades all life. All of us are trying to discover how we entered the nightmare, by what treachery we were betrayed to the storm of history. "Mother, please listen to me," cries Rowe.—"My little boy couldn't kill anyone":

[1] W. H. Auden, "New Year Letter" (1940), ll. 15–29, in *The Double Man* (1941).

His mother smiled at him in a scared way but let him talk: he was
the master of the dream now. He said, "I'm wanted for a murder
I didn't do. People want to kill me because I know too much. I'm
hiding underground, and up above the Germans are methodically
smashing London to bits all round me. You remember St. Clements
—the bells of St. Clements. They've smashed that—St. James's Picca-
dilly, the Burlington Arcade, Garland's Hotel where we stayed for
the pantomime, Maples, and John Lewis. It sounds like a thriller,
doesn't it?—but the thrillers are like life—more like life than you are,
this lawn, your sandwiches, that pine . . . it's what we've all made
of the world since you died. I'm your little Arthur who wouldn't
hurt a beetle and I'm a murderer too. The world has been remade
by William LeQueux.

Every age has its aesthetic of crime and terror, its attempt to
give form to its special psychic or neurotic climate. No age has
imposed greater handicaps on the effort than ours. Crime has
gone beyond Addison's "chink in the chain armour of civilized
communities." It has become the symptom of a radical lesion in
the stamina of humanity. The hot violence of the Elizabethans is
as different from the cold brutality of Hitlerian or Communist
Europe, the heroic sin in Aeschylus or Webster from the squalid
and endemic degeneracy in Céline or Henry Miller, the universal
proportions of Greek or Shakespearean wrong from the gratuitous
calculation and *inconséquences* of Gide's aesthetic criminals, as the
worth at which the individual life was held in those times from
its worthlessness in ours. A criminal takes his dignity from his
defiance of the intelligence or merit that surrounds him, from the
test his act imposes on the human community. He becomes trivial
when that measure is denied him. So the modern thriller is per-
mitted its prodigies of contrivance and hecatombs of death at the
cost of becoming a bore. So film audiences fidget restlessly through
the newsreel, waiting to be overwhelmed by the "edifying bilge"
of Hollywood. The thrill habit, fed by tabloids, drugstore fiction,
headlines, and events, has competed successfully with gin, drugs,
and aspirin, and doped the moral nerve of a generation.

The hardship this imposes on the artist is obvious. When felony,
by becoming political, becomes impersonal; when the *acte gratuit*
elicits not only secret but public approval, its dramatist faces the
desperate task of restoring to his readers their lost instinct of values,

the sense of human worth. It is not enough that the thriller become psychic: Freudian behavior patterns have become as much an open commodity and stock property as spy rings and torture chambers were fifty years ago. It must become moral as well.

The Victorian *frisson* of crime was all the choicer for the rigor of propriety and sentiment that hedged it in. Dickens' terrors are enhanced less by his rhetoric than by his coziness. The reversion to criminality in Dostoevsky takes place in a ramifying hierarchy of authority—family life, social caste, political and religious bureaucracy, Tzarist militarism and repression. The horror in *The Turn of the Screw* is framed by the severest decorum, taste, and inhibition. James—like Conrad, Gide, and Thomas Mann—felt the seduction of crime but he also knew its artistic conditions. "Everything you may further do will be grist to my imaginative mill," he once wrote William Roughead of Edinburgh in thanks for a book of the latter's criminal histories: "I'm not sure I enter into such matters best when they are *very* archaic or remote from our familiarities, for then the testimony to manners and morals is rather blurred for me by the *whole* barbarism. . . . The thrilling in the comparatively modern much appeals to me—for there the *special* manners and morals become queerly disclosed. . . . then go back to the dear old human and sociable murders and adulteries and forgeries in which we are so agreeably at home." The admonition might have served as the cue for the talent of Graham Greene.

Greene, dealing in a "whole barbarism" equaling or surpassing anything in history, has undertaken to redeem that dilapidation from the stupefying mechanism and inconsequence to which modern terrorism has reduced it. Arthur Calder Marshall has rightly said, in an article in *Horizon*,[2] that "few living English novelists derive more material from the daily newspaper than Graham Greene." His *mise-en-scène* includes the Nazi underground and fifth column (*The Confidential Agent, The Ministry of Fear*), Communist politics riddled by schisms and betrayals (*It's a Battlefield*), Kruger and his international swindles (*England Made Me*), Zaharoff and the alliance between munitions-making and *Machtpolitik* (*This Gun for Hire*), the English racetrack gang warfare (*Brighton Rock*), the Mexican church suppression (*The Power and*

---

[2] "The Works of Graham Greene," *Horizon*, May 1940, pp. 367-75.

the Glory), wartime in the Gold Coast (*The Heart of the Matter*), in London (*The End of the Affair*), and in Indochina (*The Quiet American*); while his *Orient Express* is the same train we've traveled on all the way from *Shanghai Express* to *Night Train* and *The Lady Vanishes*. But where once—in James, Conrad, Dostoevsky, in Dickens, Defoe and the Elizabethans—it was society, state, kingdom, world, or the universe itself that supplied the presiding order of law and justice, it is now the isolated, betrayed, but finally indestructible integrity of the individual life that must furnish that measure. Humanity, having contrived a world of mindless and psychotic brutality, reverts for survival to the test of the single man. Marked, hunted, or condemned, he may work for evil or for good, but it is his passion for a moral identity of his own that provides the nexus of values in a world that has reverted to anarchy. His lineage is familiar—Raskolnikov, Stavrogin, Kirilov; Conrad's Jim, Razumov, and Heyst; Mann's Felix Krull and Gide's Lafcadio; Hesse's Steppenwolf and Demian, and, more immediately, Kafka's K. He appears in almost every Greene novel—as hero or victim in Drover, Dr. Czinner, the nameless D., and Major Scobie; as pariah or renegade in Raven, Farrant, Rowe, and the whisky priest of *The Power and the Glory*; as the incarnation of pure malevolence in Pinkie, the boy gangster of *Brighton Rock*.

The plot that involves him is fairly consistent. *Brighton Rock* may be taken as showing it in archetype. Its conflict rests on a basic dualism of forces, saved from the prevalent danger of becoming an inflexible mechanism by Greene's skill in suggestion and insight, yet radical in its antithesis of elements. Pinkie is a believing Catholic. He knows Hell as a reality and accepts his damnation. *Corruptio optimi pessima* is the last faith left him to live or die by. Ida Arnold, the full-blown, life-loving tart whose casual lover the gang has killed, sets out to track him down: "unregenerate, a specimen of the 'natural man,' coarsely amiable, bestially kind, the most dangerous enemy to religion." She pursues him with ruthless and convinced intention, corners him, sees him killed. The boy is sped to his damnation and Ida triumphs ("God doesn't mind a bit of human nature. . . . I know the difference between Right and Wrong.") The hostility is crucial. It figures in all of Greene's mature books—Mather the detective against Raven the assassin in *This Gun for Hire*; the Inspector against Drover in *It's a Battle-*

field; the Communist police lieutenant, accompanied by the *mestizo* who acts as nemesis, against the hunted, shameless, renegade priest in *The Power and the Glory,* trailing his desecrated sanctity through the hovels and jungles of the Mexican state yet persisting in his office of grace and so embracing the doom that pursues him. It reappears in the hunting down of Major Scobie by the agent Wilson in *The Heart of the Matter,* and it counts in the tragic passion of Bendrix for Sarah Miles in *The End of the Affair.* A critic in *The New Statesman* once put the case concisely: "Mr. Greene is a Catholic, and his novel *Brighton Rock* betrays a misanthropic, almost Jansenist, contempt for the virtues that do not spring from grace." [3]

It is this grace that operates as the principle which makes palpable its necessary enemy, Evil. And it is the evil that materializes out of vice, crime, nightmare, and moral stupefaction in Greene's books that brings him into a notable company. The same evil is made to work behind the dramatic mystery and psychic confusion in *The Turn of the Screw* and beneath the squalid violence in Conrad's *The Secret Agent,* that parent classic in this field of fiction which, appearing in 1907, established the kind of novel that Greene and his generation have carried to such exorbitant lengths. To define and objectify the evil, to extricate it from the relativity of values and abstractions—arbitrary justice, impersonal humanitarianism and pity, right and wrong, good and bad— is the ultimate motive of Greene's work. His pursuit of it has carried him afield among the totems and obscenities of coastal Africa which he conjured in *Journey Without Maps,* his descent to the heart of darkness:

> It isn't a gain to have turned the witch or the masked secret dancer, the sense of supernatural evil, into the small human viciousness of the thin distinguished military gray head in Kensington Gardens with the soft lips and the eye which dwelt with dull lustre on girls and boys of a certain age. . . . They are not, after all, so far from the central darkness. . . . when one sees to what unhappiness, to what peril of extinction, centuries of cerebration have brought us, one sometimes has a curiosity to discover if one can from what we have come, to recall at which point we went astray.

An echo clearly sounds here from a passage in T. S. Eliot's essay
on Baudelaire (1930) which has become a classic statement of the
problem in recent criticism:

> So far as we are human, what we do must be either evil or good;
> so far as we do evil or good, we are human; and it is better, in a
> paradoxical way, to do evil than to do nothing: at least, we exist.
> It is true to say that the glory of man is his capacity for salvation;
> it is also true to say that his glory is his capacity for damnation.
> The worst that can be said of most of our malefactors, from states-
> men to thieves, is that they are not men enough to be damned.

And Greene has pointed to another definition of his subject in one
of the epigraphs he prefixed to his book on Mexico in 1939—a
passage, too long to quote here in full, from Newman:

> To consider the world in its length and breadth, its various his-
> tory, the many races of man, their starts, their fortunes, their
> mutual alienation, their conflicts . . . the impotent conclusion of
> long-standing facts, the tokens so faint and broken of a superin-
> tending design, the blind evolution of what turn out to be great
> powers or truth . . . the greatness and littleness of man, his far-
> reaching aims, his short duration, the curtain hung over his futurity,
> the disappointments of life, the defeat of good, the success of evil
> . . . the prevalence and intensity of sin, the pervading idolatries,
> the corruptions, the dreary hopeless irreligion, that condition of
> the whole race . . . all this is a vision to dizzy and appal; and
> inflicts upon the mind the sense of a profound mystery, which is
> absolutely beyond human solution.
>
> What shall be said to this heart-piercing, reason-bewildering fact?
> I can only answer, that either there is no Creator, or this living
> society of men is in a true sense discarded from His presence . . .
> *if* there be a God, *since* there is a God, the human race is impli-
> cated in some terrible aboriginal calamity.

The drama and present issue of that calamity are what make
the continuous theme of Greene's fiction in its development over
the past quarter-century.

II

Greene's beginnings in the novel were in a vein of romantic
Stevensonian adventure in *The Man Within,* but he emphasized

even there, in a title taken from Thomas Browne, the dualism of the moral personality ("There's another man within me that's angry with me," a derivation from Paul's "law in my members" in the Epistle to the Romans). He next applied the motif to the situation of moral anarchy in modern politics and society and began to adopt for the purpose the devices of intrigue and mystery as the modern thriller had developed them (*The Name of Action, Rumour at Nightfall, Orient Express*). These tales, at first crude and exaggerated in contrivance (Greene has dropped the first two of the last named from his collected edition), soon advanced into his characteristic kind of expertness, and all of them implied a dissatisfaction with the current tendencies in English fiction. This became explicit in his reviews of the modern novelists. Henry James, possibly Conrad, were the last masters of the English novel to preserve its powers in anything like their full tragic and moral potentialities. "After the death of Henry James," he wrote in an essay on Mauriac, "a disaster overtook the English novel: indeed long before his death one can picture that quiet, impressive, rather complacent figure, like the last survivor on a raft, gazing out over a sea scattered with wreckage."

> For [he continued] with the death of James the religious sense was lost to the English novel, and with the religious sense went the sense of the importance of the human act. It was as if the world of fiction had lost a dimension: the characters of such distinguished writers as Mrs. Virginia Woolf and Mr. E. M. Forster wandered like cardboard symbols through a world that was paper-thin. Even in one of the most materialistic of our great novelists—in Trollope— we are aware of another world against which the actions of the characters are thrown into relief. The ungainly clergyman picking his black-booted way through the mud, handling so awkwardly his umbrella, speaking of his miserable income and stumbling through a proposal of marriage, exists in a way that Mrs. Woolf's Mr. Ramsay never does, because we are aware that he exists not only to the woman he is addressing but also in a God's eye. His unimportance in the world of the senses is only matched by his enormous importance in another world.

So the novelist, taking "refuge in the subjective novel," found that he had "lost yet another dimension": "the visible world for him ceased to exist as completely as the spiritual." Mauriac accord-

ingly was rated as belonging to "the company of the great traditional novelists: he is a writer for whom the visible world has not
ceased to exist, whose characters have the solidity and importance
of men with souls to save or lose, and a writer who claims the
traditional and essential right of a novelist, to comment, to express
his views." But if Greene gave his highest honors among modern
novelists to James ("it is in the final justice of his pity, the completeness of an analysis which enabled him to pity the most shabby,
the most corrupt, of his human actors, that he ranks with the
greatest of creative writers. He is as solitary in the history of the
novel as Shakespeare in the history of poetry"), to Conrad (for his
instinct of " 'the mental degradation to which a man's intelligence
is exposed on its way through life': 'the passions of men short-
sighted in good and evil': in scattered phrases you get the memories
of a creed working like poetry through the agnostic prose"), and
to Mauriac ("if Pascal had been a novelist, we feel, this is the
method and the tone he would have used"); if he granted his
secondary respects to writers like Corvo ("he cared for nothing but
his faith . . . if he could not have Heaven, he would have Hell"),
Ford Madox Ford ("he had never really believed in human happiness"), and De La Mare ("no one can bring the natural visible
world more sharply to the eye"); if he denied the authentic creative
virtue alike to the agnostic Butler ("the perpetual need to generalize from a peculiar personal experience maimed his imagination")
or Havelock Ellis ("invincible ignorance") and to the believing
Eric Gill ("as an artist Gill gained nothing from his faith . . . his
rebellion never amounted to much") or the angry mystic Léon Bloy
("he hadn't the creative instinct . . . the hatred of life . . . prevented him from being a novelist or a mystic of the first order"),
it appeared that there was another order of talent that had conditioned Greene's own imagination from its earliest workings. He
responded to it in the adventure tales of John Buchan ("Now I saw
how thin is the protection of civilization") and Conan Doyle
("think of the sense of horror which hangs over the laurelled drive
of Upper Norwood and behind the curtains of Lower Camberwell.
. . . he made Plumstead Marshes and the Barking Level as vivid
and unfamiliar as a lesser writer would have made the mangrove
swamps of the West Coast"), but its mark had been laid on him
long before he encountered these writers: in childhood when "all

books are books of divination." Its masters then were the literary heroes of his boyhood: "Rider Haggard, Percy Westerman, Captain Brereton, or Stanley Weyman." But vividly as these ignited his imagination, much as *King Solomon's Mines* "influenced the future," it "could not finally satisfy": its characters were too much "like Platonic ideas: they were not life as one had already begun to know it." The "future for better or worse really struck" when he discovered *The Viper of Milan* by Marjorie Bowen. "It was," says Greene, "as if I had been supplied once and for all with a subject."

"Why?" he asks, and gives his answer. Here for the first time he learned that while "goodness has only once found a perfect incarnation in a human body and never will again," evil "can always find a home there"; that there is a "sense of doom" that "lies over success"; that "perfect evil walk[s] the world where perfect good can never walk again." And he acknowledges that it was Miss Bowen's Italian melodrama that gave "me my pattern—religion might later explain it in other terms, but the pattern was already there"; and after "one had lived for fourteen years in a wild jungle country without a map. . . . now the paths had been traced and naturally one had to follow them." [4]

It is apparent from these disclosures that Greene, whatever his sense of human and moral complexity or his sophisticated insight into the riddled situation of his time, early decided to address himself to a primitive order of fiction. But since the social and political conditions of the age had likewise reverted to primitive forms of violence, brutality, and anarchy he found his purpose matched in the events of the historic moment. For that moment the thriller was an obvious and logical imaginative medium, and Greene proceeded to raise it to a skill and artistry few other writers of the period, and none in English, had arrived at. His novels between 1930 and 1945 record the crisis and confusions of those years with an effect of atmosphere and moral desperation perfectly appropriate to the time. If their expert contrivance often seems to descend to sleight of hand; if the surrealism of their action and settings can result in efflorescences of sheer conjuring; if the mechanics of the thriller—chases, coincidences, strokes of accident, and ex-

[4] All these quotations are from Greene's collection of essays, *The Lost Childhood* (1951).

ploding surprises—can at times collapse into a kind of demented
catastrophe, these were not too remotely at odds with the possibilities of modern terrorism, police action, international intrigue
and violence. His superiority to the convention in which he worked
was clear; if at times it ran uncomfortably close to the jigsaw-
puzzle manipulation which entertainers like Ambler, Hammett,
and Raymond Chandler had made so readable and finally so trivial,
there was always working in it a poetry of desperation and an
instinct for the rudiments of moral conflict that lifted it to allegoric
validity. It was apparently at such validity that Greene was aiming
in these books. "What strikes the attention most in this closed
Fagin universe," he has said in writing on *Oliver Twist,* "are the
different levels of unreality"; and of Mauriac's novels he has said
that "One is never tempted to consider in detail M. Mauriac's plots.
Who can describe six months afterwards the order of events, say
in *Ce Qui Était Perdu?* . . . . We are saved or damned by our
thoughts, not by our actions."

In fiction of this kind, action itself becomes less real or representative than symbolic. Disbelief is suspended in acceptance of
the typical or the potential; incredulity yields to imaginative recognition; and since the events of modern politics and militarism
had already wrenched the contemporary imagination out of most
of its accepted habits and disciplines, Greene's plots found the
thriller fully conditioned to his purpose. If a writer like David
Cecil could say, to the charge that John Webster's plays are "ex-
travagant, irrational, and melodramatic," that "the battle of heaven
and hell cannot be convincingly conveyed in a mode of humdrum
everyday realism" and that "the wild and bloody conventions of
Elizabethan melodrama provided a most appropriate vehicle for
conveying his hell-haunted vision of human existence," a similar
defense could be argued for Greene's melodrama—the more so
because the battle of heaven and hell and the hell-haunted vision
had become part of the European and contemporary experience.

Moreover, in tales of this kind (to which the adjective "operatic,"
used by Lionel Trilling to describe certain features in the novels of
Forster, applies) character itself tends to reduce to primary or symbolic terms. The tests of average consistency or psychological realism are not of the first importance. A more radical appeal acts to
suspend them. The novel refers to something more than the prin-

ciples of temperament; the "humors" become not only moral but philosophic. At times, in books like *It's a Battlefield* and *England Made Me,* Greene worked in terms of Freudian or abnormal character types and so brought his characters into an uncomfortable but effective relation with his melodrama. At others—*This Gun for Hire* and *The Confidential Agent*—the psychic pathology submitted openly and conveniently to the claims of political violence and so left the story to rest at the level of the historical or political parable (hence "an entertainment"). In *Brighton Rock* the fable became explicitly religious; in *The Power and the Glory* it perhaps became "metaphysical" as well. The last-named novel is certainly one of Greene's finest achievements, possibly his masterpiece. In it the action and milieu are not only invested with a really convincing quality of legend. The fable itself, and the truth it evokes, are believably enacted by the two central characters—the priest with his inescapable vocation, the police lieutenant with his —in a way that is not pressed to exaggerate or simplify their primitive and symbolic functions in the drama. The book is sustained from first to last by a unity of atmosphere that harmonizes its setting, characters, moral values, and historic reference into a logical consistency of effect, and the result is one of the most haunting legends of our time.

Greene's ambition was not, however, content to rest with this kind of result. His more serious books had already aimed at being more than fables or parables. He had before him the examples of Mauriac and Faulkner, both of whom he has acknowledged as major influences in his work. *It's a Battlefield, Brighton Rock,* and *The Power and the Glory* pointed the way to a fiction of full-bodied and realistic substance, and in *The Heart of the Matter* in 1947 he undertook to write a complete and consistent novel. (His "entertainments" since that time have been frankly written for film production—*The Third Man* and *Loser Takes All.*) This brought him squarely up against the problem of reconciling his religious and didactic premises to the realistic and empirical principles of the novel form; of harmonizing an orthodoxy of belief (however personal or inquisitive) with what George Orwell once called "the most anarchical of all forms of literature." ("How many Roman Catholics have been good novelists? Even the handful one could name have usually been bad Catholics. The novel is practically a

Protestant form of art; it is a product of the free mind, the autonomous individual.")[5]

Greene certainly had no intention of conforming to the conventions of religious-literary sentimentalism. In this at least he shared what has been called "one major objective of young English Catholic writers"—"not to resemble Chesterton." On the other hand, he was by conviction committed to a belief in the efficacy and sufficiency of grace as the final test of value in character and conduct. Now that he committed himself equally to the demands of psychological and moral realism which the novel imposes, he met for the first time the tests a novelist faces when he joins the human claims of his art with the theological claims of his faith. And grace is bound to become a question-begging premise on which to rest the arguments of psychic and moral realism. ("The greatest advantage of religious faith for the artist," Gide once noted in his journal, "is that it permits him a *limitless* pride.")[6] The instinctive or lifelong believer—Mauriac, O'Faolain, Eliot, whatever their crises of "conversion" or re-conversion—usually finds a means of harmonizing orthodoxy with experience, dogma with moral inquisition. The voluntary or deliberate convert—Claudel, Greene, Waugh, perhaps Bloy and Bernanos—seems never to arrive at such reconciliation, at least not easily or convincingly. Experience and faith refuse to come to natural or practical conjunctions; in fact, it is implied that they were never intended to. Faith becomes for such men the most deadly-serious "vested interest" of their existence. If it does not assert itself in the form of a didactic or inflexible logic, it does so in the form of a perversely ingenious one. There has always been a visible gap between the writer or poet of inherited or habitual faith and the one of converted belief (the same difference shows up in writers of political dogmatism), and it is not lessened by the convert's acquaintance with unbelief. He usually conveys "the perpetual need to generalize from a peculiar personal experience," and his imagination is seldom left unmaimed, however much it may also have been stimulated.

Greene's plots from the first showed a tendency to enforce abso-

---

[5] *Inside the Whale and Other Essays* (London, 1940), p. 173.
[6] "Le plus grand advantage de la foi religieuse, pour l'artiste, c'est qu'elle lui permet un orgueil *incommensurable.*" *Journal 1889–1939*, p. 191 (5 décembre, 1905).

lutes of moral judgment—a kind of theological *vis inertiae*—which resulted in the humors to which his characters tended to reduce. The "sanctified sinner" who appears in most of Greene's books is the most prominent of these. The type has become a feature of modern religious literature. Baudelaire, Rimbaud, and Bloy (*Une Femme pauvre*) seem to have combined to give it its characteristic stamp and utility in literary mysticism, and since their day it has become a virtual cliché of religious drama and symbolism. The idea has been put bluntly by its critics: "vice is defined as the manure in which salvation flowers." [7] Orwell made a critical issue of it when he reviewed Greene's *The Heart of the Matter*.[8] It was not only the frivolity of the cult he found suspect: its suggestion "that there is something rather *distingué* in being damned" and its hint of a "weakening of belief" ("when people really believed in Hell, they were not so fond of striking graceful attitudes on its brink"). It was also its results in dramatic artistry: "by trying to clothe theological speculations in flesh and blood, it produces psychological absurdities." The cases of both Pinkie in *Brighton Rock* and Scobie in *The Heart of the Matter* were taken as showing its liabilities for a novelist: that of Pinkie by presupposing "that the most brutally stupid person can, merely by having been brought up a Catholic, be capable of great intellectual subtlety"; that of Scobie "because the two halves of him do not fit together." ("If he were capable of getting into the kind of mess that is described, he would have got into it earlier. If he really felt that adultery is mortal sin, he would stop committing it; if he persisted in it, his sense of sin would weaken. If he believed in Hell, he would not risk going there merely to spare the feelings of a couple of neurotic women.")

In other words, the arguments which such characters enact tend to become increasingly "loaded" as they advance toward explicit theological conclusions. And the fiction that embodies such arguments soon runs into the difficulty which all tendentious or didactic fiction sooner or later encounters. It no longer "argues" the problems and complexities of character in terms of psychological and moral forces; it states, decides, and solves them in terms of pre-

---

[7] Kenneth Tynan, reviewing the dramatic version of *The Power and the Glory* in *The Observer* (London), April 8, 1956, p. 11.

[8] *The New Yorker*, July 17, 1948, pp. 61–63. (See below pp. 105–9.)

established and dictated premises. Grace is always held in reserve as a principle of salvation, a principle which soon becomes too arbitrary and convenient to find justification in conduct or purpose. It descends like a Christianized *deus ex machina* to redeem its vessels when they have driven themselves into the impasse or sacrilege that would, on moral grounds alone, be sufficient to damn them. Greene of course shirks nothing in presenting his men and women as psychically complex and morally confounded. But as he advances out of parable into realism, out of the tale of violence into the drama of credible human personalities, he still keeps an ace up his sleeve, and grace is called upon to do the work that normally would be assigned to moral logic and nemesis. "O God," says Scobie after he has taken communion in a state of mortal sin and is beginning to plan his suicide, "I am the only guilty one because I've known the answers all the time." This admission of his damnation is also his plea for salvation ("I think," says the priest afterward to his widow, "from what I saw of him, that he really loved God"); and what it implies is the kind of presumption or arrogance that has become a feature of recent religious fiction: namely, that neither conduct nor morals are of final importance to the believer. *Corruptio optimi pessima:* it is not only a case of the corruption of the best being the worst. It is by their capacity for corruption or damnation that the best—the believers—qualify for redemption. "The others don't count." [9]

What accompanies this premise in Greene's later novels is likely to take a form which, whatever its theological tenability, can be as repugnant (intentionally repugnant no doubt) to normal religious feeling as it is to aesthetic judgment. "O God, I offer up my damnation to you. Take it. Use it for them," Scobie murmurs at the communion rail; and when, presently, he contemplates future repetitions of his sacrilege, he has "a sudden picture before his eyes of a bleeding face, of eyes closed by the continuous shower of blows: the punch-drunk head of God reeling sideways." On such

---

[9] Greene took for his motto of *The Heart of the Matter* a passage from Charles Péguy (subsequently shortened to its first three sentences in the published book): "Le pécheur est au coeur même de chrétienté. . . . Nul n'est aussi compétent que le pécheur en matière de chrétienté. Nul, si ce n'est le saint. Et en principe c'est le même homme. . . . C'est une cité. Un mauvais citoyen est de la cité. Un bon étranger n'en est pas." The abbreviation may be significant but the import of the whole passage is conveyed in the novel itself.

passages it is difficult not to agree with the critic who acts in re-
vulsion: "a stern theological dogma [is] grossly degraded into melodrama, to an extent which allows even a non-believer to speak of
blasphemy. . . . It is intolerable. Whether we accept the dogma
or not, it is intolerable that it should be expressed in such luridly
anthropomorphic terms as these . . . a hotting-up of religious belief for fictional purposes, a vulgarization of the faith." [10] Greene
has made a repeated point of indicting pity as a sin of presumption. Rowe, Scobie, and Bendrix are all made to suffer the consequences of assuming a divine prerogative. It is, however, hard to
believe that a similar presumption does not underlie the special
pleading that accompanies Scobie's catastrophe. "A priest only
knows the unimportant things," says Father Rank to Mrs. Scobie.
"Unimportant?" "Oh, I mean the sins," he replies impatiently.
"A man doesn't come to us and confess his virtues." To reasoning
as conveniently circular as this no practical moral appeal is
possible.

The Heart of the Matter is Greene's most ambitious book thus
far but in spite of its advance beyond the schematic pattern of its
predecessors it is not finally his most convincing one. Its excessive
manipulation keeps it from being that. *The End of the Affair* in
1951 showed an important development. It was Greene's first novel
to put aside entirely the devices of intrigue, mystery, and criminal
motivation. Its scene is modern London, its drama is intimately
personal, and though the action takes place in wartime, war does
not figure in the events except accidentally. Its plot shows a radical
simplicity, and its characters, if tormented to the point of abnormality, remain recognizable as people of credible moral responsibility. It develops a story of secret passion between a modern
novelist of brilliant sardonic talent and self-professed agnostic
egotism, Maurice Bendrix, and Sarah Miles, the suburban wife
who loves him and suffers his selfish claims to the point of immolat-
ing herself destructively to save him from death in a bombing.
Sarah makes a bargain with God: she will give up her love for
Bendrix if his life is saved. Her sacrifice brings on her the sufferings
of a religious atonement and finally results in the event of a miracle
which reveals to Bendrix the nature and consequences of his selfish

[10] Philip Toynbee, *The Observer* (London), December 4, 1955.

corruption. Greene's epigraph here comes from Bloy: "Man has places in his heart which do not yet exist, and into them enters suffering in order that they may have existence."

The tale is closely and powerfully developed, and its three principal characters are perhaps the most subtly drawn and intimately created of any in Greene's gallery. It is true that here again, especially in the final section of the book, they assume a disembodied abstraction of conduct which recalls the cases of Pinkie and Scobie, and the introduction of the miracle, shrewdly handled though it is, risks the dissolution of the entire conflict in an arbitrary conclusion. The symbolic effect that might make such an event convincing is weakened by the realistic basis on which the drama is built; it ends as the later, more schematized novels of Mauriac do, in an unprepared shift from realism to didacticism, an arbitrary change of moral (and consequently of dramatic) premises which has the effect of detaching the characters from their established logic as personalities and forcing them to serve a function outside themselves. The result is an effect of metaphysical contrivance which it would take the powers of a Dostoevsky to justify. But if Greene here resorts to an artificiality of argument that has weakened a share of Mauriac's later work, he also invites in this novel a comparison with Mauriac's psychic and moral insight. By applying himself to an intimate human conflict and laying aside the melodramatic historical framework of his earlier work, he achieves a substance that brings him to a point of renewal and fresh departure in his fiction.[11]

He remains significant, however, because of what he has done to recreate and reassert the moral necessity in his characters, and to project its reality, by symbolic means, into the human and social

---

[11] I have not included here a discussion of Greene's latest novel, *The Quiet American* of 1956. This is one of his most brilliant feats of dramatic narration, but its drama, which concerns the conflict of American and European foreign policy in the Indo-China war, though announced as representing a "new vein" in which "religion plays little or no part," amounts mainly to a transferring of his argument from a religious to a political basis. It is apparently the cynical English journalist Fowler who is equipped with political and humanitarian "grace," and the innocent, do-gooding, anti-Communist American meddler, Pyle, who is without it. "On every level except the most important one," says Philip Toynbee (an English critic), in the article already quoted, "this is a magnificent novel. But Graham Greene is a novelist who must be judged on the most important level."

crisis of his time. He has used guilt and horror for what they have signified in every age, Elizabethan, Gothic, Romantic, or Victorian —as a mode of exploring the fears, evasions, and panic that confuse men or betray the dignity of reason to violence and brutality, but which must always, whatever the historic situation in which they appear, be faced, recognized, and mastered if salvation is to escape the curse of self-deception. The identity Greene's heroes seek is that of a conscience that shirks none of the deception or confusion in their natures. If the "destructive element" of moral anarchy threatens them, it is their passion for a moral identity of their own that redeems them. It is by that passion that they give his work, to quote one of its most acute critics[12]—whatever "its intellectual dishonesty, its ellipses of approximation and selective omissions, as well as its fragmentation of character"—its "sense of history." The drama he presents, "with its evasions and its apologia, is part of our climate of fear and guilt, where it is hard for a man of good-will, lacking good actions, to see straight or to speak plain. The personal tragedy is in the womb of the general one, and pity is their common blood-stream."

It is because he dramatizes the hostile forces of anarchy and conscience, of the moral nonentity with which nature or history threatens man and the absolute tests of moral selfhood, that Greene has brought about one of the most challenging combinations of historical allegory and spiritual argument that have appeared in the present dubious phase of English fiction. His style and imagery can be as melodramatic as his action, but he has made of them an instrument for probing the temper and tragedy of the age, the perversions that have come near to wrecking it, and the stricken weathers of its soul. It still remains for him to get beyond its confusions, negative appeals, and perverse standards—not to mention the tricky arguments by which these are too often condemned in his books and which are too much left to do the work of the honest imagination—to become a fully responsible novelist in his English generation. This is a role to which his acute sense of history and his remarkable gifts in moral drama have assigned him. His skill already puts him in the descent of the modern masters—James,

[12] Donat O'Donnell, *Maria Cross: Imaginative Patterns in a Group of Modern Catholic Writers* (1952), pp. 63–91, here pp. 88–90. This book, one of the best on its subject, makes an extended analysis of *The Heart of the Matter.* . . .

Conrad, Joyce—in whom judgment and imagination achieved their richest combination, as well as in the company of the few living novelists—Mauriac, Malraux, Hemingway, Faulkner—in whom their standard survives. He is one of the few contemporary English talents who insist on being referred to that standard and who give evidence that it means to persist.

The "Trilogy"

by R. W. B. Lewis

In Greene's early fiction, along with a definite but notably uneven development of style and vigor, there was an apparent failure to distinguish between various fictional genres. Even *Brighton Rock* betrays an initial confusion between what Greene calls an "entertainment" and what he finally offered as a tragedy; but here the confusion is unexpectedly exploited (as shall be seen) in the composition of an immensely impressive novel. The distinction of genres, in a somewhat Gallic manner, would become important for Greene, and in a sense the making of him; but prior to *Brighton Rock*, we observe an uncertainty of artistic purpose that led to an unstable treatment of the basic elements of fiction: setting, character and action. Part of the success of *Brighton Rock, The Power and the Glory,* and *The Heart of the Matter* is due to the preliminary sketching of elements in each of them—a process that, as it turned out, managed to release the special energy and "vision" that would characterize Greene as a writer of stature.

The settings of *The Power and the Glory* and *The Heart of the Matter,* for example, had already been explored by Greene personally and in two excellent travel books: *The Lawless Roads,* from which whole passages are transcribed in the former; and *Journey Without Maps,* which concludes on the Gold Coast of poor Major Scobie. In the travel books, Greene's journalistic and photographic abilities exhausted themselves; and in the novels, consequently, physical settings could be managed so as to exude a meaning that transformed them into spiritual situations, into elaborated images of fate. Mexico, however discolored, is still Mexico in *The Lawless Roads*; in *The Power and the Glory,* the

"The 'Trilogy.'" From *The Picaresque Saint,* by R. W. B. Lewis (Philadelphia, Penn.: J. B. Lippincott Co., 1959), pp. 239–64. Copyright © 1956 and 1958 by R. W. B. Lewis. Reprinted by permission of J. B. Lippincott Co.

country has been reduced and reshaped to fit a particular action, of which indeed it contains the particular secret. Similarly, each one of these three novels has its correlative entertainment; a mystery story, in the popular sense, that functions ably as trial run for a mystery drama in a more ancient and theological sense. Here we touch the crucial distinction underlying the other distinctions, for the unsolvable mystery of the human condition, beyond or beneath any sociological or historical or psychological explanation thereof, has become Greene's obsessive subject. Raven, the killer in *A Gun for Sale* (1936), with his dumb conviction of injustice and his bleak yearning for a soul he can trust, is a purely human cartoon for the metaphysical monster, Pinkie, the killer of *Brighton Rock* (1938). In *The Confidential Agent* (1939), the weary and frightened fidelity to his mission of the Spanish agent, D., is a sketchy and political version of the behavior of the nameless Mexican priest, the agent of God, on his exclusively religious mission in *The Power and the Glory*, a year later. And *The Ministry of Fear* (1943), the most skillful of the entertainments and a very good story indeed, dramatizes what Greene regards as the most dangerous of human emotions— pity—the fatal flaw which would destroy Major Scobie in *The Heart of the Matter* (1948), but which is significantly contrasted in that novel with its real opposite, the primary attribute of God: mercy.

It can be said about the earlier novels, then, that the confusion of purpose and the blurry handling of the elements are rooted in a failure to disentangle the *mystery* of the mystery, to separate it out from the contingencies of melodrama and the staged surprises of the brain-twister. The disentanglement followed, as it seems, upon the Liberian experience examined above; for after that, the plot and the action of Greene's novels are increasingly given their meaning by the religious motif—a motif which, since it cannot always be called Christian, can scarcely be always called Catholic; a sort of shocked intuition of supernature. It is when the religious motif takes charge that Greene's resources—including his nervous, highly pressured style, and his uncommon talent for narrative— become ordered and controlled, and his artistic power fulfills itself.[1]

---

[1] This notion [has been developed] in rather different terms by Robert Kelly of the University of Indiana. . . . I am indebted to Mr. Kelly for several stimulating conversations about Greene.

The Man Within has an appealing youthfulness of viewpoint; but the religious element remains shadowy and generalized, and the whole story wobbles uneasily to (in context) a rather pointless climax. The real source of complexity in human events, as Greene would eventually see it, is not detected in *The Name of Action,* though that is what the novel is about; as a result, we are introduced here only to shapeless movements in a nightmare world. And in *England Made Me,* which is otherwise a genuine achievement, Greene so far misunderstood himself as to insert stream-of-consciousness meditations ill-advisedly but patently borrowed from James Joyce. Nothing could be further from Greene's intentions than those of Joyce—which achieve the careful rendering of the behavior of the mind, with the ultimate aim of celebrating the shaping power of art, the "stasis" that imposes value and meaning upon the chaos of mental experience. Greene has never reverted to the Joycean technique.[2] What Greene has envisaged and what he has become especially concerned with are better implied in the title of still another early book, *It's a Battlefield*: the human scene now described as a battlefield between transcendent warring forces. And in *Brighton Rock,* the metaphor of the battlefield is dominant: "It lay there always, the ravaged and disputed territory between the two eternities."

The three novels published between 1938 and 1948 are sometimes taken together as a trilogy; but the word should be enclosed in quotation marks, for the trilogic pattern, if it existed in Greene's awareness, took hold only belatedly. But it is worth juxtaposing the three books, to observe several striking aspects of Greene. All three show his affection for the primitive; like Silone, Greene often turns away from the relatively civilized to inspect human life in its cruder and more exposed conditions: in a dark corner of Brighton, the jungles and prisons of Tabasco, the coast of West Africa—all places where, as Scobie tells himself in *The Heart of the Matter,* "human nature hasn't had time to disguise itself"; places where there openly

---

[2] In *The End of the Affair,* the writer Maurice Bendrix, who on occasion speaks for Graham Greene, is asked about this: "You used the stream of consciousness in one of your books. Why did you abandon the method?" "Oh, I don't know," Bendrix replies in his supercilious way. "Why does one change a flat?" Because, one supposes, one does not belong there.

flourished "the injustices, the cruelties, the meanness that elsewhere
people so cleverly hushed up." In these primitive scenes, we encounter the dramatis personae of Greene's recurring drama and of
his troubled universe: the murderer, the priest, and the policeman,
who are the heroes respectively of the three books. All three figures,
in different embodiments, appear in all three novels; and they tend
more and more to resemble each other. The murderer, Pinkie, is
knowingly a hideously inverted priest; the policeman, Scobie, becomes involved with crime and criminals; the officer in *The Power
and the Glory* has "something of a priest in his intent observant
walk," while the priest in turn has queer points of resemblance with
the Yankee killer whose photograph faces his in the police station.
The three figures represent, of course, the shifting and interwoven
attributes of the Greenean man: a being capable of imitating both
Christ and Judas; a person who is at once the pursuer and the man
pursued; a creature with the splendid potentiality either of damnation or salvation. The actualities of their fate exhaust, apparently,
the major possibilities. If one can be sure of anything in the real
world or in Greene's world, Pinkie Brown is damned—it is his special mode of triumph; the Mexican priest is saved—sainthood
gleams at last through his bloodshot eyes; and the final end of
Major Scobie is what is precisely in doubt, as difficult to determine
as his own ambiguous last words, "Dear God, I love. . . ." Pinkie
is a proud citizen of hell; Scobie's suffering is that of a man in
purgatory; and the laughter in *The Power and the Glory* celebrates,
perhaps, the entrance of a soul into paradise. The three careers are
presented to us in three very different kinds of fiction: *Brighton
Rock* just manages to escape melodrama and becomes a work *sui
generis; The Power and the Glory* is, in its way, a divine comedy;
and *The Heart of the Matter* is a tragedy in the classical tradition.
These novels are, respectively, Greene's most strenuous, his most
satisfying, and, artistically, his most assured.

Brighton Rock in particular is the most harrowing of Greene's
stories about children; and Pinkie, the seventeen-year-old gangster
(he is usually referred to simply as "the Boy") is "the most driven
and 'damned' " of all Greene's characters, to quote his own words
about the evil forces in that other fearful tale about children,
James's *The Turn of the Screw*. There is, to be sure, a superficial
movement in the novel from death to life: the narrative begins

with the revenge-murder by Brighton race-track hoodlums of Hale,
the man who is working a publicity stunt for a newspaper among
the holiday crowds; and it closes with the pregnancy of Rose, the
wan underage wife whom Hale's killer, Pinkie, has been forced for
protection to marry. So far, there is a momentary likeness to
Moravia's *Woman of Rome,* which similarly concludes with the
heroine's pregnancy by a now dead murderer. Moravia's novel quite
definitely suggests the painful victory of life over death. But
Greene's artistic and intellectual purposes are almost always dialec-
tically opposite to those of Moravia; and in *Brighton Rock,* not
only is the death legally avenged, the birth itself will be altogether
darkened by Rose's discovery of Pinkie's true feeling about her—
via the "loving message" he has recorded by phonograph, and which,
"the worst horror of all," she is on her way to hear as the story
ends: "God damn you, you little bitch, why can't you go back home
for ever and let me be?"[3] The implied denouement in *Brighton
Rock* is as disagreeable as anything in modern fiction. But *Brighton
Rock* is deliberately pitiless, and partly because it aims, by moving
beyond human pity, to evoke the far faint light of an incomprehensible divine mercy.

Part of the disaster that threatens in this pitiless book is artistic:
a threat to the shape and character of the book itself. Greene evidently began it as an "entertainment," and the first American edition announced itself as such. He began it, that is, as a melodrama
of murder and detection in which contingency and coincidence
would be allowed free play, the chase be exciting for its own sake,
and with a larger and more kindly emphasis than the novel eventually allowed on Ida Arnold, the London lady of easy virtue who
had known Hale in his last frightened hours and who sets herself
to discover the criminal, an aim she formidably succeeds in. But
evil has always stimulated Greene a good deal more than the right-
ing of wrongs; and in this case, the figure and story of Pinkie Brown

---

[*] The film version of *Brighton Rock,* so I am told, introduced a suggestive
change in the matter of the phonograph record. The words recorded by Pinkie
in the film go something like this: "You may think I love you, but to me you
are just an ugly brat, and I hate you." When Rose plays the record (a moment
left to our appalled imagination in the book), the needle sticks in the groove,
and the voice is heard saying, "You may think I love you I love you I love you
. . ." It is a device that hints at the mixture of loathing and attraction that the
bewildered Pinkie feels.

(unlike those of Raven in *A Gun for Sale,* of which *Brighton Rock* would otherwise have been a repetition) expanded in Greene's imagination until a recognizable tragedy took its place in the book alongside the well-made entertainment. The entertainment is Ida's; it begins with the first sentence ("Hale knew, before he had been in Brighton three hours, that they meant to murder him"), and ends with the police closing in on the culprit. The tragedy is Pinkie's; *it* begins more subtly in the atmosphere of the place (implied by the adjectives used for the jostling crowds: "bewildered," "determined," "cramped," "closed," "weary"); and its action is defined in advance by the book's motto, from *The Witch of Edmonton,* with overtones of *Macbeth*: "This were a fine reign:/To do ill and not hear of it again." In the open world of the entertainment, happenstances accumulate; but in the tragedy there is no space for contingency, no time for the accidental. Evil is fertile and is always heard from again; every move Pinkie makes—from the killing of Hale, through the further necessitated murders and the detested courtship and marriage, to the climax in which, like Oedipus, he blinds himself (with vitriol)—has a convulsive inevitability, the more dreadful since it seems rooted neither in private temperament nor in social background. It derives from the inexplicable power of evil, one of the two things that Pinkie believes in: *"Credo in unum Satanum."* *Brighton Rock* confirms Greene's statement in the preface to a book about him by the French critic, Paul Rostenne, that he has no a priori edifying purpose in writing his novels, but is carried along rather by the unpredictable energies of his characters. As Pinkie's perils increase and his ambitions enlarge, the very design of the book shifts and re-forms.

Brighton Rock could have been a kind of disaster, two different books, between the same covers only by mistake. But it emerges as an original and striking work: for the relation between the detective story and the tragedy expresses exactly what *Brighton Rock* is finally all about. It is a relation between modes of narrative discourse that reflects a relation between two kinds or levels of reality: a relation between incommensurable and hostile forces; between incompatible worlds; between the moral world of right and wrong, to which Ida constantly and confidently appeals, and the theological world of good and evil inhabited by Pinkie and Rose. It is, in short, the relation Greene had formulated for himself in Liberia, between the "sinless empty graceless chromium world" of modern Western urban civilization and the supernaturally infested jungle with its purer terrors and its keener pleasures. The abrupt superiority of *Brighton Rock* to anything Greene had yet written comes from the fact that for the first time he had separated the mystery from the mystery and confronted the one with the other.

Here, of course, the confrontation takes the form of deadly warfare: "She [Ida] stared out over the red and green lights, the heavy traffic of her battlefield, laying her plans, marshalling her cannon fodder." That sense of the universal drama is both ancient and modern; for *Brighton Rock,* to put the case in perhaps exaggerated and misleading theological terms, belongs with the early and late medieval tradition, the tradition now again in fashion: the tradition of Tertullian and the dark, negative, and incorrigibly paradoxical theology wherein everything supernatural stands in implacable hostility over against everything natural and human; and for the most part, vice versa. This is the view Albert Camus has identified and attacked as *the* Christian tradition. But in another tradition, in so-called theocentric humanism, there are intermediate ends, intermediate goods, and intermediate explanations: because there is an intermediate figure, the God-man, Christ, who reconciles the realms and makes sense out of human history. But about Pinkie and his small explosive world, there is nothing intermediate—here everything is sudden and ultimate.[4] Pinkie has no great involvement with the things of this world, with money or with sexual love or even with Brighton. His Brighton is not a town or a "background" but a Fury-driven situation; and he is involved immediately with evil and catastrophe.

He is deeply implicated, too, of course, with good—with the forlorn waitress Rose, who has just enough information about Hale's murder to make Pinkie decide savagely to marry her in order to keep her quiet; and who is as doomed to salvation (that is how Greene prefers to describe it) as Pinkie is to damnation. He sees her as his necessary counterpart. "What was most evil in him

[4] Miss Frances Ebstein, a former student of mine, has quoted Heidegger suggestively to say of Pinkie that he was not so much born and bred as "ejaculated into existence."

needed her; it couldn't get along without her goodness. . . . Again
he got the sense that she completed him." Their world, too, is a
battlefield, but with a difference:

> Good and evil lived together in the same country, spoke the same
> language, came together like old friends, feeling the same comple-
> tion, touching hands beside the iron bedstead. . . . [Their] world
> lay there always, the ravaged and disputed territory between two
> eternities. They faced each other as it were from opposing terri-
> tories, but like troops at Christmas time they fraternised.[5]

In *Brighton Rock,* the theme of companionship, which takes so
many forms in the fiction of the second generation, appears as the
reluctant fellowship between good and evil and is symbolized in the
illegal marriage of Pinkie and Rose and the uncertain sexual union
of the two virgins on their wedding night. There, touching hands
beside the iron bedstead, they peer out together at the "glare and
open world," the utterly alien world of Ida Arnold. "She was as
far from either of them as she was from Hell—or Heaven."

In Ida's world, the religious impulse is softened into a comfortable moralism; but in Pinkie's world, the human impulse shrivels
and looks ugly. Pinkie sees only extreme alternatives—not even
sacred and profane love, for example, but the supernatural and the
obscene. Normal love is reduced to the pornographic, and is opposed only by fidelity to supernature; here, as in *England Made
Me,* religion becomes a substitute for or even a heightened form of
pornography. Pinkie quotes venomously from the cheap literature,
"the kind you buy under the counter. Spicer used to get them.
About girls being beaten." But in choosing the alternative, in submitting to the supernatural, Pinkie attaches himself primarily to
supernatural evil. *"Credo in unum Satanum"* is the violent admission elicited on the same page by the outburst against pornography;
and though he tells Rose scornfully, "Of course there's Hell," about
heaven he can only say "Maybe."

As Pinkie pursues his dream of damnation, the tragic dimension
of *Brighton Rock* turns into a sort of saint's life in reverse. The
seven sections of the book dramatize one by one an inversion of all

[5] The image of enemy troops fraternizing is widespread in contemporary fiction. It recurs in *The Heart of the Matter,* is an actual event and a key experience in Malraux's *Les Noyers de l'Altenberg,* and is elaborated into book-
length allegory in Faulkner's *A Fable.*

or most of the seven sacraments, dramatize what we might call the seven deadly sacraments:[6] as Pinkie is confirmed in the habit of murder ("Hell lay about him in his infancy. He was ready for more deaths"), is ordained as a priest of his satanic church ("When I was a kid, I swore I'd be a priest. . . . What's wrong with being a priest? They know what's what"), performs the act of matrimony (which here is a mortal sin), and receives the vitriolic unction in the moment of his death. The entire reversal accomplished in *Brighton Rock,* haphazard though it is, manages to dignify the repellent protagonist on the principle indicated to Rose, at the very end, by the sniffling old priest: *Corruptio optimi est pessima.* The worst is the corruption of the best; only the potentially very good can become so very evil, and only the sacraments that save can so effectively become the sacraments that blast.

Despite its singularly uninviting character, accordingly, the narrow and oppressive world of Pinkie Brown is clearly to be honored —in the terms of the novel—over the spiritual bourgeoisie of Ida Arnold. Her world, for all its robust good humor, is increasingly represented as sterile, and she as a hollow, heartless menace. Ida, with her big breasts and her warm enveloping body, remains childless; it is the angular, nearly sexless Rose who conceives at once, after a single sexual venture. And the final worldly victory of Ida, her destruction of Pinkie, coincides with a hidden defeat of her own world: a repudiation of it, accomplished relentlessly by the rhetoric of the book. That rhetoric aims at separating out and then destroying the moral domain, in the name of the theological; the conventional values of right and wrong are lured into prominence and then annihilated. This is done by a series of seeming contradictions that sometimes appear strained and perverse, but often make arresting similes. A remark about Pinkie—"his virginity straightened in him like sex"—aptly suggests the colliding opposites that animate his experience. Oxymorons are employed in the account of Ida and her behavior, and with the intention of transforming or "transvaluating" our judgment of her. When allusion is made to Ida's "remorseless optimism" or her "merciless compassion," the aim is to negate the familiar human attributes—in

---

[6] I am indebted to Mr. Herbert Haber, a former student of mine, for this phrase and for working out in detail a theory we shared about the structure of *Brighton Rock.*

this case, cheerfulness and pity—by stressing their remoteness from the religious virtues: in this case, penitent humility and mercy. The adjective, from its higher plane, denies all value to the nouns on their lower human level. And the whole process culminates in the epilogue when the priest, coughing and whistling through the grille in that unattractive and seedy way Greene's priests almost always have, says to Rose about Pinkie—destroyed now by the ferocious pity of Ida Arnold—that no human being can conceive "the appalling strangeness of the mercy of God."

About this verbal technique, which may best be defined as a technique of befuddlement and concerning which one has the uneasy suspicion of mere cleverness, there will be more to say. Meanwhile, it is to be noted that as the detective story and the tragedy intertwine in *Brighton Rock,* we find ourselves in a universe wherein seeming opposites—good and evil—become closely allied, and seeming likenesses—the good and the right—are totally opposed. These paradoxes, too, are incarnate in the central figure. Pinkie, Greene's first memorable image of the character he had so cherished as a boy in *The Viper of Milan*—"perfect evil walking the world where perfect good can never walk again"—is a replica of Judas who none the less has faint confusing echoes about him of the perfectly good, of Christ. He is the worst *only* by virtue of being the corruption of the best. And so, when his unstable associate Cubitt is talking about him to Ida and when Cubitt denies being a friend of his—" 'You a friend of Pinkie's?' Ida Arnold asked. 'Christ, no,' Cubitt said and took some more whiskey"—there is the fleeting whisper of a memory: "A court-yard, a sewing wench beside the fire, the cock crowing." And Cubitt goes on to deny him thrice.

On numerous occasions Greene has quoted the lines from Æ's poem, "Germinal":

> In ancient shadows and twilights
>   Where childhood had strayed,
> The world's great sorrows were born
>   And its heroes were made.
> In the lost boyhood of Judas
>   Christ was betrayed.

It is not only the realm of supernatural good and its unlikely representative Rose which are betrayed by the lost boyhood of this demonic Judas; it is also the flickers of the Christ in himself. It is within such a context and by such insinuations that Greene earns Pinkie the right to be regarded, as though reflected in a crazy-mirror on Brighton pier, as an image of the tragic hero. There can be no doubt, finally, about the damnation of Pinkie Brown: except the enormous doubt that, according to Greene, must attend our every human judgment and prediction.

The motto of *The Power and the Glory* is from Dryden: "Th' inclosure narrow'd; the sagacious power/Of hounds and death drew nearer every hour." The lines could apply to *Brighton Rock* and with a little stretching to *The Man Within,* as well as to most of Greene's entertainments; they summarize Greene's settled view of human experience. But they are peculiarly appropriate to *The Power and the Glory,* which is, one could say, Greene's most peculiarly appropriate novel and which comprises the adventures of a hunted man—the last Catholic priest in a totalitarian Mexican state—whom the hounds of power catch up with and to whom death does come by a firing squad. There is no complication of genres here: the novel has a single hero and a single action—and both are strikingly representative of the special kind of hero and heroic adventure that characterize the fiction of the second generation.

According to the laws of the godless Mexican state, the priest is an outlaw simply because he carries on his priestly duties; but he has also broken the laws of his Church. He is a rogue, a *picaro,* in several kinds of ways; his contradictory character includes much of the comical unpredictability of the traditional *picaro;* and the narrative Greene has written about him is perhaps the most patently picaresque of any we are considering—the lively story of the rogue on his travels, or better, on his undignified flights from and toward the forces of destruction. In no other novel of our time, moreover, are the paradoxes of sainthood more expertly handled. The priest—who is a slovenly drunkard and the father of a devilish little child, who giggles a good deal and is often helplessly weak at the knees—is also a potential, perhaps finally an actual saint. He feels at the end that he has failed: "It seemed to him, at that moment, that it would have been quite easy to have been a saint. . . . He felt like someone who has missed happiness at an ap-

pointed place." But other evidence throughout the book suggests
that all unwittingly he had kept his appointment with beatitude.
The Power and the Glory stands beside Silone's *Bread and Wine*.
And the so-called "whiskey-priest," disguised as a layman and
fumbling his way toward disaster, is, if not the twin, at least a
brother of Pietro Spina, a layman (a revolutionist) disguised as a
priest, and similarly the last lonely witness to truth in his own
neighborhood, who is equally pursued by the forces of oppression
and who is likewise the attractive, incompetent, and saintly source
of damage and of death to almost everyone involved with him.
These two novels give the most revealing account in second generation fiction of the hero as outlaw, fleeing and transcending the
various forms that power currently assumes.

In terms of Greene's artistic and intellectual development, however, another motto, in place of Dryden's, might be drawn from the
book itself: when the priest, heading bumpily into the hills of
Tabasco on mule-back, daydreams in the imagery of a "simplified
mythology"—"Michael dressed in armour slew the dragon, and the
angels fell through space like comets with beautiful streaming hair
because they were jealous, so one of the Fathers had said, of what
God intended for men—the enormous privilege of life—this life."
This Life. In this novel, by a refreshing contrast with *England
Made Me* and *Brighton Rock,* the religious impulse no longer
denigrates and undermines the human but serves rather to find
in it or to introduce into it a kind of beauty and a kind of goodness. "I tell you that heaven is here," the priest cries out to the
vacant-faced peasants gathered dumbly in a hut on the mountain-
side at dawn. It is, of course, characteristic of Greene that, in *The
Power and the Glory,* where the divine image for once irradiates
and redeems the human, it is seen doing so only to the most squalid,
repellent and pain-racked of human conditions—just as omens of
sanctity are seen only in an unshaven brandy-bibber. Natural
beauty is not enhanced, but natural ugliness is touched by grace.

> At the centre of his own faith there always stood the convincing
> mystery—that we were made in God's image—God was the parent,
> but He was also the policeman, the criminal, the priest, the maniac
> and the judge. Something resembling God dangled from the gibbet
> or went into odd attitudes before the bullets in a prison yard or
> contorted itself like a camel in the attitude of sex. He would sit in

the confessional and hear the complicated dirty ingenuities which God's image had thought out: and God's image shook now, up and down on the mule's back, with the yellow teeth sticking out over the lower lip, and God's image did its despairing act of rebellion with Maria in the hut among the rats.

Characteristically, too, it is less the splendor than the almost ridiculous *mystery* of the thing that Greene wants to dramatize. But let him do so in his own manner: in *The Power and the Glory* a compassionate and ultimately a very charitable manner. For it is by seeking God and by finding Him in the darkness and stench of prisons, among the sinners and the rats and the rascals, that the whiskey-priest arrives at the richest emotion second generation fiction has to offer: the feeling of companionship, and especially the companionship of the commonly guilty and wretched. Arrested for carrying brandy, crowded into a pitch-black cell, crushed between unseen odorous bodies, with a woman on one side hysterically demanding to make her trivial confession and an unseen couple copulating somewhere on the floor, announcing their orgasms with whimpering cries of pleasure, the priest is touched suddenly "by an extraordinary affection. He was just one criminal among a herd of criminals. . . . He had a sense of companionship which he had never experienced in the old days when pious people came kissing his black cotton glove."

To appreciate this scene—it is the whole of chapter three of part two, and in my opinion the most effective scene Greene has yet written—we should locate it in the structure of the novel. It begins a few pages beyond the mathematical center of the book; but it constitutes the center as well of an action that has its clear beginning and its firmly established end. The basic unit in the structure of *The Power and the Glory* is the encounter: as it is in so many other novels of the second generation with their picaresque tendency and their vision of man as an outlaw wandering or hastening through an anarchic and hostile world. In *The Power and the Glory*, as in *Bread and Wine*, the plot is episodic and consists of a succession of encounters between the harried protagonist and a number of unrelated persons—while within that succession, we observe a pattern of three dominant and crucially meaningful encounters.

We first see the priest when, in disguise, he sips brandy in the

office of Mr. Tench, the morose expatriate dentist. We follow him,
episode by episode, as he is hidden and given food by Coral, the
precocious daughter of an agent for a banana company, Captain
Fellowes, and his miserable death-haunted wife; as he arrives in
the village which is the home of the woman, Maria, by whom he
has had the child Brigitta; as he travels onward in the company of
a mestizo, the yellow-toothed ignoble Judas who will betray him
to the police; as he is arrested and released and fights his way over
the mountains to freedom in a neighboring state and the comfortable home of Mr. Lehr and his sister, German-Americans from
Pittsburgh, in charge of a mining operation; as he is enticed back
across the border of Tabasco to attend the death of James Calver,
an American murderer who has been fatally wounded by the police;
is arrested again by the police lieutenant, taken back to the capital
city, and executed. Tench, Coral, Maria, the Lehrs, Calver: these
are all strangers to each other. The episodes with each of them
thicken and expand the novelistic design (Coral, for instance, is the
priest's good spiritual daughter, while Brigitta is his evil actual
daughter). But the design itself is created by the three encounters
between the priest and the lieutenant.

These occur at carefully spaced intervals, about one third and
two thirds through the book, and then at length in the climax. The
first time, the lieutenant—whose whole energy and authority are
directed exclusively to capturing this last remaining agent of the
Church—sees the priest and interrogates him; but he neither recognizes nor arrests him. The second time, the priest is arrested, but
he is not recognized: the charge is carrying liquor. The third time,
recognition is complete and the arrest final. But these encounters
are mere indicators of a carefully constructed plot; the action is
something different and more telling, and we are made conscious
of it from the outset when—in separate, successive views of them—
paradoxical resemblances are registered about the two men. The
priest disappears wearily into the interior, giving up a chance to
escape in order to minister to a sick peasant woman and feeling
"like the King of a West African tribe, the slave of his people, who
may not even lie down in case the winds should fail." On the next
page, the lieutenant marches by with a ragged squad of police,
looking as though "he might have been chained to them unwillingly: perhaps the scar on his jaw was the relic of an escape." Later,

as he walks home alone, dreaming of a new world of justice and well-being for the children of Tabasco, "there was something of a priest in his intent observant walk—a theologian going back over the errors of the past to destroy them again." The exhausted and sometimes drunken soldier of God, the chaste and fiercely dedicated priest of the godless society: each one enslaved to his mission, doomed to his role and its outcome: these are the beings, the systole and diastole, between whom the force of the novel is generated.

Readers of Dostoevski or of the Book of Revelation will easily identify them. They are the "hot" and the "cold" bespoken by the angel in lines quoted twice in *The Possessed*: "These things saith the Amen . . . I know thy works, that thou art neither cold nor hot: I would thou wert cold or hot. So then, because thou art lukewarm, and neither cold nor hot, I will spue thee out of my mouth" (Revelation III, 14–16). The lieutenant has had the chilling vision of absurdity: "He was a mystic, too, and what he had experienced was a vacancy—a complete certainty in the existence of a dying, cooling world, of human beings who had evolved from animals for no purpose at all. . . . He believed against the evidence of his senses in the cold empty ether spaces." With a devotion only to the reality of the here and now, he is a rebel against all the misery and injustice and unhappiness he associates with the rule of a greedy Church and its insistence on the unimportance of the human lot in this world. He watches the children in the street, his love for them hidden beneath his hatred of the Church and its priests: "He would eliminate from their childhood everything which had made him miserable, all that was poor, superstitious and corrupt."

The lieutenant, in a word, is *l'homme révolté* of Albert Camus, seen—with respect—in the unorthodox religious perspective of Graham Greene. François Mauriac was right, in his preface to the French édition of *The Power and the Glory*, to call the novel an answer in narrative terms to the widespread European sense of absurdity—to that sense as somehow the one necessary prerequisite to the struggle for social justice. *The Power and the Glory* is not perhaps *the* answer; but it does contain, among other things, a potent allegory of one of the major intellectual debates of our time. Greene, too, it should be said, gives fairer and more substantial play to what he regards as the opposition—embodied in the lieutenant—than Camus gives to *his* opponent, the crudely drawn cleric Paneloux in *The Plague*. Camus contrasts Pameloux, and his helpless appeal to divine irrationality, with the rational and dignified Rieux and Tarrou; while Greene joins the upright police officer in a contest with the wavering and incompetent whiskey-priest. Yet the nameless priest, consecrating moistly amidst the unspeakable heat and the detonating beetles of Tabasco, sweating his way toward a sort of befuddled glory, is of course the representative of the "hot," and the lieutenant's proper adversary.

These two are the persons of stature in the universe of the novel, and eventually they acknowledge each other. "You're a good man," the priest says in astonishment when, at the moment of his release from prison, the lieutenant gives him five pesos. And: "You aren't a bad fellow," the lieutenant concedes grudgingly, during the long conversations after the final arrest. Most of the other characters, those whom Greene calls "the bystanders," are the lukewarm, and their artistic purpose is, by a variety of contrasts, to illuminate the nature of the hunt. A good many of the more "regular" members of the Church, in fact, both in the past and now in the pleasant safety of another state, appear as lukewarm; *The Power and the Glory* may be a religious novel, but it is decidedly not an ecclesiastical one. The priest himself had been lukewarm in the old days, going smugly on his parochial rounds and attending the meetings of the guilds. It is only in his moment of degradation, arrested not even for being the last priest with the courage to remain in Tabasco but only as a common citizen carrying contraband, that the priest reveals the "hot," the heroic side. He does so unconsciously, out of humility and a conviction of his own unworthiness and an irrepressible sense of humor. We return to the prison scene mentioned above: it occurs just before the second of the three major encounters.

The whole of it should be studied, from the entrance into the cell to the departure next morning and the sudden sense of companionship even with the lieutenant. But perhaps the following fragments can suggest the remarkable interplay—not, in this case, the remote opposition—of sacred and obscene love, of beauty and extreme ugliness, of comedy and deadly peril: all of which gives the scene a rich multiplicity of action beyond anything Greene had previously achieved. Just as the key moment in *Bread and*

Wine occurs in the darkness of a squalid hut, so here the "epiphany" takes place in the blackness and stench of a prison.

> Among the furtive movements came again the muffled painless cries. He realised with horror that pleasure was going on even in this crowded darkness. Again he put out his foot and began to edge his way inch by inch from the grill.
> "They'll shoot you, father," the woman's voice said.
> "Yes."
> "Are you afraid?"
> "Yes. Of course."
> A new voice spoke, in the corner from which the sounds of pleasure had come. It said roughly and obstinately, "A man isn't afraid of a thing like that."
> "No?" the priest asked.
> "A bit of pain. What do you expect? It has to come."
> "All the same," the priest said, "I *am* afraid."
> "Toothache is worse."
> "We can't all be brave men." [7]
> The voice said with contempt, "You believers are all the same. Christianity makes you cowards."
> "Yes. Perhaps you are right. You see I am a bad priest and a bad man. To die in a state of mortal sin"—he gave an uneasy chuckle—"it makes you think."

*   *   *

> A long train of thought began, which led him to announce after a while, "They are offering a reward for me. Five hundred, six hundred pesos, I'm not sure." Then he was silent again. He couldn't urge any man to inform against him—that would be tempting him to sin—but at the same time, if there was an informer here, there was no reason why the wretched creature should be bilked of his reward. To commit so ugly a sin—it must count as murder—and to have no compensation in this world. . . . He thought: it wouldn't be fair.
> "Nobody here," a voice said, "wants their blood money."
> Again he was touched by an extraordinary affection. He was just one criminal among a herd of criminals. . . . He had a sense of companionship which he had never experienced in the old days,

[7] Greene achieves a telling effect, for those who remember this particular interchange, when at the end, the description of the execution is juxtaposed with a picture of the chief of police moaning cravenly over his aching tooth in the dentist's office.

when pious people came kissing his black cotton glove.

The pious woman's voice leapt hysterically out at him. "It's so stupid to tell them that. You don't know the sort of wretches who are here, father. Thieves, murderers. . . ."

"Well," an angry voice said, "why are you here?"

"I had good books in my house," she announced, with unbearable pride. He had done nothing to shake her complacency. He said, "They are everywhere. It's no different here."

"Good books?"

He giggled. "No, no. Thieves, murderers. . . . Oh, well, my child, if you had more experience, you would know there are worse things to be."

*   *   *

Somewhere against the far wall pleasure began again: it was unmistakeable: the movements, the breathlessness, and then the cry. The pious woman said aloud with fury, "Why won't they stop it? The brutes, the animals!"

"What's the good of your saying an Act of Contrition now in this state of mind?"

"But the ugliness. . . ."

"Don't believe that. It's dangerous. Because suddenly we discover that our sins have so much beauty."

"Beauty," she said with disgust. "Here. In this cell. With strangers all around."

"Such a lot of beauty. Saints talk about the beauty of suffering. Well, we are not saints, you and I. Suffering to us is just ugly. Stench and crowding and pain. *That* is beautiful in that corner—to them. It needs a lot of learning to see things with a saint's eye: a saint gets a subtle taste for beauty and can look down on poor ignorant palates like theirs. But we can't afford to."

"It's a mortal sin."

"We don't know. It may be. But I'm a bad priest, you see. I know—from experience—how much beauty Satan carried down with him when he fell. Nobody ever said the fallen angels were the ugly ones. Oh no, they were just as quick and light and . . ."

Again the cry came, an expression of intolerable pleasure. The woman said, "Stop them. It's a scandal." He felt fingers on his knees, grasping, digging. He said, "We're all fellow prisoners. I want drink at this moment more than anything, more than God. That's a sin too."

"Now," the woman said, "I can see you're a bad priest. I wouldn't believe it before. I do now. You sympathise with these animals. If your Bishop heard you . . ."

"Ah, he's a very long way off." He thought of the old man now —in the capital: living in one of those ugly comfortable pious houses, full of images and holy pictures, saying Mass on Sundays at one of the Cathedral altars.

"When I get out of here, I shall write . . ."

He couldn't help laughing: she had no sense of change at all. He said, "If he gets the letter he'll be interested—to hear I'm alive."

Pinkie Brown and Major Scobie, the protagonists of *Brighton Rock* and *The Heart of the Matter,* are never seen to smile, much less to laugh; the former is in a constant state of fury, the latter of apprehension. It is the laughter, almost more than anything else, that distinguishes *The Power and the Glory*: laughter based on the recognition of God's image in man, evoked by the preposterous incongruity of it and yet leading naturally to a warmth of fellow-feeling. Here again, a similarity may be noted with the comedy and the companionship of *Bread and Wine*; and perhaps Silone was not wrong, after all, to turn the ridiculous Sciatàp of that novel into the treacherous figure of *The Seed Beneath the Snow.* In this particular comic vision, even the traitors—even the Judases—have a clownish aspect. Contemplating the mestizo (in another passage) and recognizing him as a Judas, Greene's priest remembers a Holy Week carnival where a stuffed Judas was hanged from the belfry and pelted with bits of tin: "it seemed to him a good thing that the world's traitor should be made a figure of fun. It was too easy otherwise to idealise him as a man who fought with God—a Prometheus, a noble victim in a hopeless war" (the very archetype, in short, of Camus's rebel). But the force of the comic consciousness in *The Power and the Glory* is indicated, properly enough, at the end, when the lieutenant, having completed his mission and arranged for the priest's execution, sits down at his desk and falls asleep. "He couldn't remember afterwards anything of his dream except laughter, laughter all the time, and a long passage in which he could find no door." It is the lieutenant, Greene suggests, who is the trapped man, the prisoner; and the laughter he hears is like that laughter recorded by Dante on the upper slopes of purgatory, the chorus celebrating the release of a captive human soul from punishment and its entrance into paradise.

The priest himself hears none of that laughter and goes to his death persuaded of practical and spiritual failure: "I don't know a thing about the mercy of God," he tells the lieutenant, in the phrase that also rounds out *Brighton Rock* and *The Heart of the Matter*; ". . . But I do know this—that if there's ever been a single man in this state damned, then I'll be damned too. . . . I wouldn't want it any different." It never occurs to the priest that if he should so far honor the mestizo as to call him a Judas, he might himself appear as a version of the man Judas betrayed. The book has been hinting as much all along, in the pattern and style of the priest's adventures. The relationship is far more pressing and elaborate here than in *Brighton Rock* or *The Heart of the Matter,* where the vigor of supernature is hardly sweetened by the figure of inter- mediary and reconciler. The priest, accordingly, preaches to the poor and the meek and downtrodden across the hilly countryside; is tempted in the wilderness; is betrayed, tried, and executed. Toward the end, he, too, is juxtaposed with a common criminal— the Yankee killer, whose name, James Calver, echoes two syllables of the mount on which Christ was crucified, and opposite whose picture in the prison office there is a picture of the priest, grinning within the halo someone had inked around the face for identifica- tion. There is even a kind of resurrection in the little epilogue— about which one has mixed feelings—when a new, frightened priest arrives in town and is greeted with reverence by the boy Juan, who, prior to the martyrdom, had been a disciple of the lieutenant. That epilogue, offering presumably the first of the priest's miracles after death, insists perhaps too much. But if the priest is associated not only with Christ but with non-Christian divinities—the god-king of an African tribe, and the surrogate for the god, the bull that was slaughtered in the early Greek ritual of sacrifice and rebirth ("Then there was a single shot . . . the bull was dead")—the entire pattern is nevertheless artistically redeemed by a full awareness of the grotesque disproportion between the model and its re-enact- ment. "The priest giggled: he couldn't stop himself. He said, 'I don't think martyrs are like this.'" It is the giggle that saves both the priest and the novel Greene has written about him. For it is when he laughs that we know this slovenly rogue, this unshaven *pícaro,* to be also a saint; and we know that here for once—as in only one or two other novels—the paradoxes have held firm and the immense delicate balance has been maintained.

The Heart of the Matter is the most traditional of Greene's novels, in both content and construction. As such, it is obviously less representative than *The Power and the Glory*; and as such, it has a special appeal for those who mean by the word *novel* the kind of work that was typical in the nineteenth century. We note a major paradox about second generation writers: they are developing a rather new sort of fiction—the novel as an act of inquiry or of rebellion or of expiation, rather than as a direct and unprejudiced impression of life; but at the same time, most of them turn for support not to the experimental achievements of the first generation but to the literary forms of the nineteenth century. The paradox is further strained in the case of *The Heart of the Matter*. Here, for example, is the careful delineation, not altogether unworthy of Trollope, of various discordant elements in a multicolored society, the society of the coastal city in West Africa that Greene had known on his journey in 1935 and again as a government official during the war in 1942–43, the date of the novel's action.[8] In *The Heart of the Matter*, there is no savage eruption out of animal holes into the glare and open world that characterized *Brighton Rock*, and none of the rhythmic peregrinations through anarchy of *The Power and the Glory*. The incidents take place very much *within* the society of the book and involve—not proscribed outlaws but—persons of significance and authority whose intimate knowledge of each other provides much of the hero's tragic dilemma. Here, too, there is a narrative pace, leisurely but never slack, reminiscent of Greene's distant relation, Robert Louis Stevenson. Greene may not be a master of all the elements of fiction, but that he is a master of narrative can be doubted only by those too little interested in storytelling to be capable of discrimination; *The Heart of the Matter* is very handsomely told.

---

[8] Greene felt about Trollope, it will be recalled, that his characters *existed* with added force, since they existed not only for each other "but also in a God's eye." This is the sense he tries to impart to the members of this novel's society. "Here you could love human beings nearly as God loved them, knowing the worst."

And here, too, is an array of characters in the old tradition—and including one especially, the merchant Yusef, whose fat and candid dishonesty would have pleased Dickens and even more, Wilkie Collins. Here, in short, is a traditional, almost a conventional *novel* that is yet a novel by Graham Greene, and something the nineteenth century could scarcely have imagined. For what the action serves to expose is not the habits of a society or the nature of the human heart (no one, says Father Rank in the epilogue, knows "what goes on in a single human heart"); but, going beyond all that, the absolute mystery of the individual destiny.

"Why, why did he have to make such a mess of things?" This is the hopeless and embittered question raised on the last page by Major Scobie's wife, Louise: not "Why did he?" but "Why did he *have to?*" That Scobie, the late Assistant Commissioner of Police, had made an appalling mess of things cannot be denied. *The Heart of the Matter* is the progressive account of it, from the first moment when he is passed over for promotion, through the disappointment of his restless, vaguely artistic wife—a disappointment so great that Scobie makes a dubious if not illegal transaction with the diamond-smuggler, Yusef, to get enough money to send her on a trip to South Africa; through the adulterous affair with the schoolgirlish widow, Helen Rolt, on which he embarks during his wife's absence; through the now rapid deterioration of his public and private life; through the agony—for a Catholic of his temperament—of receiving the sacrament in a condition of mortal sin; to the still graver sin of despair and suicide by which Scobie ends his career. The mess is so great and Scobie's talent, at every turn, for making bad matters worse is so remarkable that the novel has occasionally been dismissed as implausible. George Orwell once wrote to the effect that no one who could get into such deep trouble so quickly could ever have had the honorable career Scobie is alleged to have had in the first place. In the sane and skeptical humanism of Orwell, the contention is reasonable; but it is a point made outside the world of the book; within that world, the issue of plausibility does not arise.

As a matter of fact, the novel offers a definite though still typically mysterious answer to Louise Scobie's question. It would not have satisfied Orwell, for it is not drawn, finally, from psychology: that, Greene thinks, is not where the real mystery lies. But, before approaching the real mystery, it should be said that *The Heart of the Matter* does also offer clues for a purely psychological explanation of Scobie and his conduct. He has the ingredients of a genuine tragic hero. He is presented as a good man, rather better than most, with an inviolable sense of justice irritating to some of his colleagues. "You're a terrible fellow, Scobie," the commissioner tells him affectionately. "Scobie the Just." He is an able man and within limits a forceful one; and he is a strong Catholic with that special religious intensity that only Greene's Catholics (not, that is, the Catholics one thought one knew) betray. And he has a fatal flaw: but it is not arrogance or any normal form of pride; Scobie calls down ruin on himself, plainly and articulately, but not through *hubris*. His flaw is an excess of the quality Greene calls pity—an inability to watch disappointment or suffering in others—with this portion perhaps of pride (in Greene's view), that he feels it peculiarly incumbent upon himself to relieve the pain. In *The Ministry of Fear*, the entertaining trial run for *The Heart of the Matter*, Arthur Rowe's troubles begin when he commits a mercy killing—or, to stick to Greene's verbal distinctions, a "pity-killing"—to end the intolerable physical suffering of his wife. Scobie kills no one, though he feels himself implicated in several deaths; like some other heroes of second generation fiction, it is his misfortune to harm most of those he longs to help or even to save.

Scobie's troubles begin with his attempt to alleviate the painful disappointment of his wife. His feeling of guilt about her is due partly to his failure to be promoted; but it is rooted more deeply in another failure, an inability any longer to love his wife; and it goes back, too, to the moment when Scobie was unable to be present at the death of his child. He is a man clearly given to self-accusation, and the pattern of it thickens as the story moves forward. It might well be that the suicide, a third of the way through, of Dick Pemberton—an assistant district commissioner at Bamba who hangs himself and whose mode of death affects Scobie enormously—may have released in Scobie a congenital self-destructive impulse.[9] Pemberton's name, Dicky, with which he signed the suicide note, and the nickname Louise has coyly pinned on her husband—Ticki (his real name is Henry)—blur in Scobie's mind

[9] This notion is interestingly proposed by Marie-Béatrice Mesnet in *Graham Greene and the heart of the matter* (London, 1954).

while he lies ill with fever after the Pemberton affair; and from then on, the pace of his decline grows more rapid. Scobie, in summary, is an affecting human being, whose sorry career is all too understandable. He is burdened by his own habit of pity for others. But we can ally ourselves with him in that other kind of pity that Aristotle called one of the two emotions properly evoked by tragedy. Still, it is the second of the emotions named by Aristotle —the emotion of tragic terror—that is the more deeply aroused in us by this novel, according to Greene's intention. Tragic pity (to borrow Joyce's definitions of these ancient terms) associates us with the human sufferer, during his grave and terrible experience. Tragic terror springs rather from our stimulated awareness of the secret cause of the suffering; and in *The Heart of the Matter,* as traditionally, that secret cause is the action of God.

The "heart of the matter," as a phrase, occurs after the opening of the novel's second part, when Scobie, momentarily alone and looking up at the stars, wonders whether "If one knew . . . would one have to feel pity even for the planets? if one reached what they called the heart of the matter?" Less than ten minutes later, unknowingly—though he does suddenly feel cold and strange—Scobie reaches the heart of the matter and gives up the peace of his own soul. Coming in from his reverie, into the resthouse where they have brought the stretcher-cases from a torpedoed ship, Scobie is asked to stand watch over two victims who lie unconscious on two beds divided by a screen. One is a six-year-old girl. Looking at her, Scobie thinks again of his own dead daughter; and he begins to pray. "Father . . . give her peace. Take away my peace for ever, but give her peace." We are to understand, I believe, that God does exactly that. He gives the child the peace of death and a release from suffering, and Scobie's peace is taken away for the remainder of his earthly career. This is the book's major turning point, when pity deepens into terror. And the human agent through whom God acts is the patient on the other side of the screen, "the young woman lying unconscious on her back, still grasping the stamp-album." It is Helen Rolt, whom pity and loneliness will drive Scobie to make love to, in an affair that so torments Scobie's Catholic conscience that only an overdose of tablets can rescue him.

Here, as in *The End of the Affair* and *The Potting Shed,* God moves in a singularly Mephistophelean manner, His wonders to

perform—a deity with whom one bargains away one's peace or love
or beliefs, or the life of someone else. In a letter to the French
Christian existentialist Marcel Moré, Greene put Scobie's case
plainly enough: "Obviously one did have in mind that when he
offered up his peace for the child it was genuine prayer and had the
results that followed. I always believe that such prayers, though
obviously a God would not fulfill them to the limit of robbing him
of a peace for ever, are answered up to the point as a kind of test
of a man's sincerity and to see whether in fact the offer was merely
based on emotion." [10] Literary criticism does not invite us to
scruple over Greene's religious orthodoxy or lack of it; our concern is simply the dramatic effectiveness of any religious opinion he
happens to show. On this ground, *The Heart of the Matter* should
be reckoned as successful precisely by implying a terrible tension
between the divine and the human—a somber and disturbing modern version of the Greek tragic tension between fate and freedom.
As in almost everything Greene has written except *The Power and
the Glory,* the supernatural power and the human religious impulse work against the purely human inclination: even when the
result is an awe-inspiring fulfillment, the granting of a wish. We
may be dismayed that things are seen to be happening so, but that
they are seen dramatically cannot be doubted.

Greek classical tragedy customarily ended by a choral acknowl-
edgment of the unsolvable mystery and the purgatorial terror.
Father Rank performs a similar function in *The Heart of the Matter,* in the epilogue Greene has characteristically added to ensure
our befuddlement over the exact meaning of the events. "For goodness' sake, Mrs. Scobie, don't imagine you—or I—know a thing
about God's mercy. . . . The Church knows all the rules. But it
doesn't know what goes on in a single human heart." Again, the
institutionalized Church is opposed in the name of the religious
mystery; and again, the sheer incomprehensibility of God's mercy
and grace is the aspect insisted upon. Again, too, the hero, moving
doggedly toward disaster, is oddly associated with the figure of
Christ: in the manner of *Brighton Rock* rather than *The Power and
the Glory,* for we are once more in a universe without intermedi-
aries. The role of Judas is played out by the English government

[10] Quoted by Marie-Béatrice Mesnet, *ibid.,* p. 102.

spy, Wilson, who covets Scobie's wife as well as his reputation for integrity; and Scobie tries desperately to condone his act of despair by seeing in it an imitation of Christ: "Christ had not been murdered: Christ had killed himself: he had hung himself on the Cross as surely as Pemberton from the picture rail"—a notion that turns up again after the suicide in *The Living Room*. All these items provide the reader, as planned, with a full measure of uncertainty about Scobie's conduct in this world and his chances in the next. It is suggested in the last lines that Scobie may really have loved God; and it is suggested that God may be the only being he did love. The night before he encounters the dying child and Helen Rolt, we hear Scobie murmuring the incomplete phrase as he falls asleep, "O God, bless—," and later, another incomplete phrase as he falls senseless and dying: "Dear God, I love . . ." Not even the reader, who knows more about Scobie than anyone else, can be sure of the objects of those verbs.

Psychology thus yields to a dark theology, the pity to the terror, the human sufferer to the secret cause. All we are meant to know is that we know nothing; that is the answer to Louise's question. Pinkie Brown *almost* certainly is damned, and he was without any doubt a vicious and wicked young man. The Mexican priest is almost certainly saved, and he was one of the most curiously sympathetic figures in modern fiction. We conclude, about Henry Scobie, in a purging sense of the unguessable nature of human conduct and divine intervention. In so far as they do constitute a trilogy, Greene's three novels reverse the direction of the greatest religious trilogy, *The Divine Comedy*. Dante's poem moves from ignorance to knowledge, from discord to harmony, from unspeakable darkness to overwhelming light. Greene's "trilogy" moves stealthily deeper into the darkness, moves through the annihilation of our confidence in human knowledge to an awareness of impenetrable mystery, moves from the deceptive light to the queerly nourishing obscurity. All the truth of things, for Greene, lies hidden in the darkness: whether of slum-ridden Brighton, of a squalid prison cell, or of a West African night of wonder and despair. Scarcely less mysterious is Greene's achievement of making visible in that darkness, and exactly by means of it, the unforgettable dramas of extraordinarily living human beings.

Graham Greene

by François Mauriac

The work of an English Catholic novelist—of an Englishman returning to Catholicism—like *The Power and the Glory* by Graham Greene, at first always gives me the sensation of being in a foreign land. To be sure, I find there my spiritual country, and it is into the heart of a familiar mystery that Graham Greene introduces me. But everything takes place as though I were penetrating into an old estate through a concealed door unknown to me, hidden in a wall covered with ivy, and as though I were advancing behind the hero of a novel through tangled branches and suddenly recognized the great avenue of the park where I played when I was a child and deciphered my initials cut on the trunk of an oak on some former holiday.

A French Catholic enters the church by the main door only; he is interwoven with its official history; he has taken part in all the debates which have torn it throughout the centuries and which have divided the Gallican church especially. In everything he writes, one discovers at once whether he is on the side of Port-Royal or the Jesuits, whether he weds Bossuet's quarrel with Fénélon, whether he is on the side of Lamennais and Lacordaire or if it is with Louis Veuillot that he agrees. Bernanos' work of which it is impossible not to think on reading *The Power and the Glory* is very significant in this respect. All the Catholic controversies of the last four centuries unfold in filigree. Behind the Abbé Donissan of the *Sun of Satan,* appears the curate of Ars. Bernanos' saints, like his liberal priests and like the pious laymen he describes with such happy ferocity, betray his venerations and his hatreds.

Graham Greene, himself, broke, like a burglar, into the kingdom of the unknown, into the kingdom of nature and of Grace. No prejudice troubles his vision. No current of ideas turns him aside from that discovery, that key which he found suddenly. He has no preconceived notion of what we call a bad priest; it could be said that he has no model of saintliness in his mind. There is corrupted nature and omnipotent Grace; there is poverty-stricken man who is nothing, even in evil, and there is mysterious love which lays hold upon him in the thick of his ridiculous misery and absurd shame to make a saint and martyr of him.

The power and the glory of the Father burst forth in the Mexican curate who loves alcohol too much and who gets one of his parishioners pregnant. A type so common and mediocre that his mortal sins call forth only derision and a shrugging of the shoulders, and he knows it. What this extraordinary book shows us is, if I dare say so, the utilization of sin by Grace. This priest, rebellious and condemned to death by the public authorities and on whose head there is a price (the drama takes place in a Mexico given over to atheistic and persecuting rulers), who tries to save himself, as indeed all the other priests, even the most virtuous, did, who in fact saves himself and passes the frontier, but who comes back every time a dying person needs him, even when he believes his help will be in vain, and even when he is not ignorant that it is a trap and that the one who is calling him has already betrayed him, this priest, a drunkard, impure and trembling before death, gives his life without for a single moment losing the feeling of his baseness and his shame. He would think it a joke if he were told he was a saint. He is miraculously saved from pride, complacency and self-righteousness. He goes to his martyrdom, having always in his mind the vision of the soiled nothingness and the sacrilege that a priest in a state of mortal sin is, so that he sacrifices himself on attributing to God all of that power and glory which triumph over what he considers the most miserable of men: himself.

And as he approaches the end, we see this mediocre sinner conform slowly to the Christ until he resembles Him, but that is not saying enough: until he identifies himself with his Lord and his God. Passion begins again around this victim chosen from among human derelicts, who repeats what Christ did, not as at the altar,

without it costing him anything, on offering the blood and the
body under the species of bread and wine, but giving up his own
flesh and blood as on a cross. [In this false, bad priest it is not
virtue that appears as the opposite of sin, it is faith—faith in that
sign he received the day of his ordination, in the trust that he
alone (since all the other priests have been massacred or have fled)
still bears in his hands, unworthy but yet consecrated.]

[The last priest remaining in the country, he is unable not to
believe that after him there will be no one to offer the Sacrifice,
or to absolve, or to distribute the bread which is no longer bread,
or to help the dying on the threshold of life eternal. And yet his
faith does not waver, although he does not know that scarcely
will he have fallen when another priest will suddenly and fur-
tively appear.

We feel it is that hidden presence of God in an atheistic world,
that subterranean flowing of Grace which dazzles Graham Greene
much more than the majestic façade which the temporal Church
still erects above the peoples. If there is a Christian whom the
crumbling of the invisible Church would not disturb, it is, indeed,
that Graham Greene whom I heard at Brussels evoking, before
thousands of Belgian Catholics, and in the presence of a dreaming apostolic nuncio, the last pope of a totally dechristianized
Europe, standing in line at the commissary, dressed in a spotted
gabardine, and holding in his hand, on which still shone the
Fisherman's ring, a cardboard valise.

That is to say that this book is addressed providentially to a
generation that the absurdity of a crazy world is clutching by the
throat. To the young contemporaries of Camus and Sartre, desperate prey to an absurd liberty, Graham Greene will reveal, perhaps, that this absurdity is in truth only that of boundless love.

The message is addressed to believers, to the virtuous, to those
who do not doubt their merit and who have ever present in their
minds several models of holiness, with the proper technic for
attaining the various steps in the mystical ascension. It is addressed in particular to Christian priests and laymen, especially to
writers who preach the cross but of whom it is not enough to say
they are not crucified. A great lesson given to those obsessed with
perfection, and those scrupulous people who split hairs over their
shortcomings, and who forget that, in the last day, according to

the word of Saint John of the Cross, it is on love that they will be judged.

Dear Graham Greene to whom I am attached by so many bonds, and first of all by those of gratitude (since thanks to you, my books to-day find the same warm reception in England that they received in my own country, at the time that I was a happy young author), how pleasant it is for me to think that France, where your work is already loved, is going to discover, thanks to that great book, *The Power and the Glory,* its true meaning. That state which you describe, which tracks down the last priest and assassinates him, is indeed the very one we see arising under our eyes. It is the hour of the Prince of this world, but you paint him without hatred. Even the executioners, even your chief of police is marked by you with a sign of mercy; they search for truth; they believe, like our communists, they have found it and are serving it—that truth which demands the sacrifice of consecrated creatures. Darkness covers all the earth you describe, but what a burning ray crosses it! Whatever happens, we know we must not be afraid; you remind us that the inexplicable will be explained and that there remains a grating to be put up against this absurd world. Through you, we know the adorable limit to the liberty that Sartre grants to men; we know that a creature loved as much as we are has no other liberty than that of refusing that love, to the degree to which it has made itself known to him and under the appearances it has been pleased to assume.

The Force of Caricature

*Aspects of the art of Graham Greene, with particular
reference to* The Power and the Glory

by Richard Hoggart

Admirers of Graham Greene usually reserve a special place
for *The Power and the Glory,* the story of a priest's flight through
a land which has forsaken the Faith. I have in mind not so much
specialists and critics as the large number of people who normally
read few novels and yet are devoted readers of Graham Greene.
Why should this novel be so highly regarded? Does it possess some
typical qualities in stronger measure than Greene's other books?
Are the theme, the manner or the setting particularly attractive,
and if so why?

Setting is always important and constitutive in Graham Greene,
but in *The Power and the Glory* even more than elsewhere. The
theme is indivisibly priest-and-land, his journey through a country
against whose condition, simply by being what he is, he makes a
charge. The land is given over to a "huge abandonment"; it rolls
through time "like a burning and abandoned ship." Variations on
these phrases echo throughout the book. So far as this country likes
to think itself modern, it has chosen the sterile progressivism of
the police lieutenant; so far as it is what it always was, though now
without acknowledging its condition, it is "a landscape of terror
and lust." Here the echoes are even more insistent: this is a world
"of treachery, violence and lust," of "violence everywhere . . . was
there no end to violence"; this is the land of the corrupt and
cowardly Jefe, of the fang-toothed Judas ("they [the priest and the

Judas] might have been the only survivors of a world which was
dying out"), of a whole people who "carried the visible marks of the
dying about with them."

But the darkness is occasionally illuminated by evidence of grace,
by the courage of the girl Coral, by the unwillingness of his fellow-
prisoners to betray the priest after he has made himself and the
price on his head known, by the lieutenant's gift of money to help
the unrecognized priest on his way. [The priest is a whisky-priest, a
coward, the father of a child born of his loneliness and weakness, a
once arrogant man who quickly recovers his old attitudes when he
reaches safety.] Yet, "after all . . . he carries on," says a minor
character; he carries on, continually touched by conscience, and
finally goes back from safety to administer the last sacrament to a
dying murderer, knowing the call to be a trap. After his execution
a new priest follows in the abandoned land.

One could scarcely miss the allegory. I say allegory rather than
symbolism to indicate a manipulation of the material in accordance
with a view of the world which the writer has from outside that
material, so to speak. I reserve symbolism for a more inward em-
bodiment of the writer's attitude to experience, in which the attitude does not so much precede the creation of the fiction as find
itself in the fiction. I would therefore apply the adjective "symbolic" to Kafka's novels but not to *The Power and the Glory*.

This society is clearly our society, allegorically heightened:
"This place [the prison] was very like the world: overcrowded with
lust and crime and unhappy love; it stank to Heaven. . . ." This
is our world, as it presents itself to Graham Greene: corrupt but
denying sin; man-centred but still in the presence of God. The
primary characteristics of Greene's view of the world are unhappiness and sin; it is "stinking to heaven," the priest repeats, and later,
"the world's unhappy whether you're rich or poor." [One believes
in God and original sin, to begin with, because not to believe
would be to find the whole situation meaninglessly cruel.] The long
and frequently quoted passage from Cardinal Newman which
forms the motto to *The Lawless Roads* (the quarry for *The Power
and the Glory*) makes the general point most clearly, ending:

> What shall be said to this heart-piercing, reason-bewildering fact
> [of evil in the world]? I can only answer, that either there is no
> Creator, or this living society of men is in a true sense discarded

from His presence . . . *if* there be a God, *since* there is a God, the human race is implicated in some terrible aboriginal calamity.

Greene gives the personal application on the third page of *The Lawless Roads*:

And so faith came to one—shapelessly, without dogma, a presence above a croquet lawn, something associated with violence, cruelty, evil across the way. One began to believe in heaven because one believed in hell, but for a long while it was only hell one could picture with a certain intimacy.

Seedy settings attract because there one sees life as it really is, with none of the thin platforms over the abyss which normal social life constructs. Speaking in *The Lost Childhood* of the blitzed cities, Greene says: "That, I think, is why one feels at home in London or in Liverpool or Bristol . . . because life there is what it ought to be." One cannot fail to see there the vast struggle which is for ever being played out in human existence. Greene's vision of the world is intensely dramatic—it alternates between the rubbish tip at the far end of the town and the outer stars, between Father José the apostate priest, standing in his nightshirt in his miserable compound, laughed at by the boys and called for by his gross wife, and the galaxies towards which his hands ineffectually gesture.

Hell is certainly pictured with a certain intimacy, with more intimacy than heaven, than the instances of goodness and love. They are included, are recognized intellectually, but do not seem to be felt anywhere near as strongly as the wickedness. Indeed, Greene sometimes finds only sinfulness where many of us would find something less reprehensible. Ida, the fat Guinness-and-oysters barmaid of *Brighton Rock*, who has clearly all kinds of virtues, even though she may not recognize sin and will go on talking about right-and-wrong, is several times directly and violently disparaged by Greene. I think particularly of the way he vilifies her as she prepares to spend the night in an hotel with Phil Corkery. Or of his comment on the workers who come in thousands for a day at Brighton, people very like Ida: "Her amusements were their amusements, her superstitions their superstitions . . . she had no more love for anyone than they had."

It is the last clause which grates, which is—one's own experience of life insists, and without being simply a jolly humanist—just not the whole truth. Greene has misunderstood; his obsession has blinded him to an important part of the truth. So it is also as the priest in *The Power and the Glory* sits at the side of the dying murderer. The murderer knows, and thinks the priest does not, that the call to the deathbed is a trap, and spends his last few minutes trying to persuade the priest to take his revolver and escape, cursing "the bastards" who have laid the trap. Immediately after the death of the gunman the priest prays, " 'O merciful God, after all he was thinking of me, it was for my sake . . .' but he prayed without conviction. At the best, it was only one criminal trying to aid the escape of another—whichever way you looked there wasn't much merit in either of them." The priest presumably prays "without much conviction" because, in terms of doctrine, confession for the gunman is the only relevant action at this moment, and his refusal to confess a final refusal of grace. But both the interpretations of the attitude which is preventing the gunman from making the act of confession are unconvincing. He was not likely to be prompted simply by unselfish thought for the priest or simply by the wish of one criminal "to aid the escape of another." His response was probably lower than the former, but certainly higher than the latter. "The bastards" is partly an angry moral assertion against the lowness of the trick, and not therefore to be dismissed so flatly.

What Greene does seem to feel very strongly for others is not so much love as pity. The history of Scobie, in *The Heart of the Matter,* is the history of a man drawn to his death by overweening pity. For Greene knows—it accounts for much of the ambiguity in his relation to his characters—that "pity can corrupt," as Auden said of his work. Yet Greene can never still the promptings of pity. It is surely this which causes him, whenever his characters are particularly reduced, to slip into the imagery of lost children . . . Loo and Anthony at the end of their short-lived relationship in *England Made Me,* or Mr. and Mrs. Fellows at the beginning of *The Power and the Glory*: "There was no meaning anywhere outside their hearts; they were carried like children in a coach through the huge spaces without any knowledge of their destination." And later in the bedroom of the capital's only hotel, after the death of

Coral: "They gave an odd effect of being children, lost in a strange town, without adult care."

This world of Greene's is presented in such vivid allegory, is so obviously intensely felt, that for a time we find it absorbing. At the back of our minds, becoming more insistent as we re-read, questions about it thrust themselves upon us. But perhaps our doubts about the nature of Greene's world and our interest in the sources of his novels' appeal are really aspects of the same question. If so, we should be able, by a detailed textual examination, to discover something not only about the technical bases of their attraction, but also about the connection between Greene's way of writing and his outlook on experience.

Greene's style is nervous, vivid, astringent, the vehicle of a restless and pungent imagination: it picks out the shopkeeper in the Lehrs' village with his "three commercial chins"; the "hooded and cramped pleasure" of the act of sex in prison; the mean-spirited, self-righteous sisters leaving jail in the early morning, "they were both tied up in black shawls like things bought in the market, things hard and dry and second-hand"; and the director of Private Tutorials Ltd., "Henry Beckley, B.A."—the name presents him at once . . . a third in English at Oxford; behind the shiny rimless glasses a bright "let me be your father" smile; an incipient predatory hardening of the mouth which would like to be charming. Or one recalls the effect of the word "bastard" on the priest, catching at his heart like the name of someone you love heard in a strange company; or the creation of the atmosphere of collapse in heat and disillusion in the very first paragraph as Mr. Tench, the ruined dentist, goes out hopelessly for the ether cylinder he's bound to miss getting.

These are in themselves important qualities, and need only to be recalled. Yet their effect over any length is of something overgeneralized and rhetorical. On looking more closely one finds that the epithets, for instance, are often either unusually arresting or just cliché—"patience" is likely to be either "monstrous patience" or simply "stony patience." The emotions are being pulled out of shape, put into overbold relief: Mr. Tench had been seized by the desire to be a dentist after finding a discarded cast in a wastepaper basket, "Fate had struck. . . . We should be thankful we cannot see the horrors and degradations lying around our childhood, in cupboards and bookshelves, everywhere": Coral feels the first pains of menstruation, "The child stood in her woman's pain and looked at them: a horrible novelty enclosed her whole morning: it was as if today everything was memorable" (and why should it be only "horrible"?—Greene seems almost to hate the physical aspects of sex): the mother of the priest's child speaks about her, "She said 'She's bad through and through.' He was aware of faith dying out between the bed and the door." Or one remembers the water-pipes which gurgle through Greene's novels. Like the Wurlitzer organ—"the world's wet mouth lamenting over life"—they are among the telltale voices of modern civilization, this time of the individual's loneliness behind all the mechanics. Anthony, the wastrel ex-public-schoolboy in *England Made Me,* tries to make yet another anonymous hotel bedroom look friendly: "He stood in the middle of the room wondering what to do next to make the room look like home, listening to the hot-water pipes wailing behind the wall." In *The Power and the Glory,* the water-pipes play a sad background music to the scene, again in an hotel bedroom, in which the priest's communion wine is drunk for him, "somewhere in the distance a pipe gurgled and the beetles detonated against a bare globe."

Greene uses the selectively typical catalogue as much as Auden, partly because they naturally tend to handle their material similarly, partly because they both began to write in the Thirties when reportage made the catalogue very popular. More importantly, it seems to me, Greene's use of the catalogue follows from his way of looking at life. If life is seen as a vast pattern then all the details of life can easily become parts of the pattern; they can be "placed" with a certain sureness and inevitability. At its best the manner is illuminating; at its worst it can suggest a kind of contempt, as though the author is saying, "One knows that people such as these will always dress like this, have this kind of house, this kind of furniture." On the reader the effect may be quietly flattering, though, of course, the author may not intend this. The reader may appear to be invited to collaborate by the suggestion that he, like the author, has seen this kind of thing before; nothing is unexpected to the wide eye of the intelligentsia. This is the detail you

will expect to find, it seems to say, if you are one of the cognoscenti;
the items are typical of a whole genre.[1] For instance, the cheap
bookie's house in *Brighton Rock*:

> He looked with contempt down the narrow hall—the shell-case
> converted into an umbrella stand, the moth-eaten stag's head bear-
> ing on one horn a bowler hat, a steel helmet used for ferns. . . .
> He lit the gas fire, turned on a stand lamp in a red silk shade with
> a bobble fringe. The light glowed on a silver-plated biscuit box, a
> framed wedding-group.

The garage of the gimcrack villa where Pinkie hides:

> A spade, a rusty lawn-mower, and all the junk the owner had
> no room for in the tiny house: an old rocking horse, a pram
> which had been converted into a wheelbarrow, a pile of ancient
> records: "Alexander's Rag Time Band," "Pack up your Troubles,"
> "If you were the only Girl"; they lay with the trowels, with what
> was left of the crazy paving, a doll with one glass eye and a dress
> soiled with mould.

Anthony undressing in *England Made Me*:

> . . . the rather torn photograph of Annette which he had stripped
> from its frame (he leant it against his tooth mug), the ties which
> he had crammed into his pocket at the lodgings, his new pants,
> his new vests, his new socks, *The Four Just Men* in a Tauchnitz
> edition, his dark blue pyjamas, a copy of *Film Fun*. He turned out
> his pockets: a pencil, a half-crown fountain pen, an empty card-case,
> a packet of De Reszke cigarettes.

Or the empty Fellows' bungalow in *The Power and the Glory*:

> He looked in through the window—perhaps this was the child's
> room. Everything had been removed from it except the useless or
> the broken. There was a cardboard box full of torn paper and a
> small chair which had lost a leg. There was a large nail in the white-
> washed wall where a mirror perhaps had been hung—or a picture.
> There was a broken shoe-horn. . . . The priest opened the door
> on the left—perhaps it had been the bedroom. In a corner lay a
> pile of old medicine bottles: small fingers of crudely coloured liquid
> lay in some of them. There were medicines for headaches, stomach-
> aches, medicines to be taken after meals and before meals. Some-

---

[1] Sir G. Rostrevor Hamilton has discussed the use of this kind of catalogue
in *The Tell-Tale Article: A Critical Approach to Modern Poetry* (1949).

body must have been very ill to need so many? There was a hair-brush, broken, a ball of hair-combings—very fair hair turning dusty white.

The detail is acutely observed, but is all too typical—we are in the world of *New Statesman* competitions.

Greene's similes are almost always short and sharply juxtapose the concrete, actual or temporal with the abstract, subjective or eternal. They can therefore have a genuine and important function in an allegory. But some of them seem to have been written by rote, and there are so many that the cumulative effect is dulling. These are some from *The Power and the Glory* only:

Evil ran like malaria in his veins.
The memory was like a hand, pulling away the past, exposing him.
Heat stood in the room like an enemy.
She carried her responsibilities carefully like crockery across the hot yard [of Coral].
The old life peeled away like a label.
He could feel his prayers weigh him down like undigested food.
Pride wavered in his voice, like a plant with shallow roots.

Sometimes the abstract/concrete relationship is reversed:

It was like hate on a death-bed [of a dog's snarl].
He drank the brandy down like damnation.

The repeated three-steps-down ending gives the effect of a flat "not with a bang but a whimper," hopeless, corner-of-the-mouth tailing-off.

This was what he was used to: the words not striking home, the hurried close, the expectation of pain coming between him and his faith.

You cannot control what you love—you watch it driving recklessly towards the broken bridge, the torn-up track, the horror of seventy years ahead.

Their little shameless voices filled the patio, and he smiled humbly and sketched small gestures for silence, and there was no respect anywhere left for him in his home, in the town, in the whole abandoned star.

The effect of all these stylistic qualities is of repeated jabs from a hypodermic syringe, of overforcing, of distortion, of a boldly caricaturish manner.

The narrative of *The Power and the Glory* derives its undoubted force from three main structural features: (i) the extreme simplicity of the overall pattern, and the skill and complexity with which the themes are interwoven through its three parts; (ii) the striking visual quality of the scenes; (iii) the speed of transition between those scenes. Henry James said that he composed his novels dramatically; one could say that Greene composes his cinematically. The construction here could hardly be simpler; the parts deal respectively with the setting and the arrival of the priest; the pursuit to its apparent end in safety; and the return, the execution and the arrival of the new priest. Indeed, the pattern is too neat; the new priest comes too pat on his cue, becomes a mechanical metaphor for the assertion that the Faith goes on and the horror is always repeated.

Throughout, the eye shifts constantly, without explanatory links. In the first paragraph the solitary figure of Mr. Tench is picked up crossing the hot deserted square; a few vultures look down at him; he tosses something off the road at them and one rises; with it goes the camera and introduces us to the town, the river, the sea. As the paragraph closes we drop to Mr. Tench again, now at the far side of the plaza, and now in his setting. Thereafter the camera moves from the dentist to the police-chief, to the pious woman reading, to the Fellows. The process is repeated with variations in the last chapter; the execution is presented as it *affects* the minor characters, and only seen, not through the narrator, but through the eyes of Mr. Tench as he looks from the window of his dingy surgery, whilst the Jefe moans with fright in the chair. Greene can assume an audience familiar with unusual camera angles and quick fadings in and out, and uses both with great skill.

The power of the individual scenes comes primarily from Greene's ability to see them in the most striking way, to know how to place them and where to let the light fall—as when the priest and a mangy dog circle a rotten bone, or when the priest turns back. At that point a mule is ready to take him forward to full safety; Miss Lehr stands ready to give a good missionary's "godspeed"; the half-caste has arrived with his story which the priest recognizes as a lie but cannot refute. There is a moment in which he stands between the two, between safety and death; only he knows all that is happening. The moment is held, and then—the mule is wheeled about and the priest sets off back.

The predilection for striking juxtaposition which informs Greene's similes is given extended exercise in the composition of scenes. The pious mother reads the silly literary life of a martyr as the hunt starts for one she rejects as a bad priest but who will be martyred; at the close the same situation is picked up again—she is reading yet another literary martyrdom as the real one takes place not far away. The priest, dirty and exhausted in the South American heat, shelters from the savage pursuit in the Fellows' deserted bungalow, and reads with difficulty Coral's English literature test paper:

> *I come from haunts of coot and hern . . .*

This rapid alternation of stripped narrative and highly-charged scene is, I think, the second main cause of Greene's attraction. He presents everything visually heightened, and with immense deftness. But his manner of composition promotes over-excitement, is not sufficiently complex and qualified. He never bores; he rarely even taxes. This is structure as caricature.

Greene's characters have a kind of intense nervous life which at first almost convinces but is soon seen to be breathed into them by Greene's breath, and always by his breath. They surprise us, as the scenic juxtaposition surprises us, but they surprise so regularly and neatly that they eventually fail to surprise. They are flat characters given a series of twists; they are revolved rapidly or stood on their heads at intervals; but when one has mastered the direction of the twist and the timing of its recurrence the pattern is exposed and there is no more surprise. We do not take it any longer for more than set movements with a wooden figure. So the priest, in spite of the great skill that has gone to make him, is no more than an intensely felt idea presented through a puppet. He seems to come to odd life at intervals, but we soon cease to regard it as anything other than one of the puppet's regular reactions. In tight corners he almost invariably gives a surprised giggle—"a little gulp of astonished laughter"—at some inconsequential memory. The lieutenant's appearance of life comes from the tension between the cold progressive on top and the wish to love underneath, which reveals itself occasionally in unexpected actions, like the giving of a coin to the priest as he dismisses him from prison. But again, the over-management kills, as in the lieutenant's inexpressible emotion and his gesture with the hands in these extracts; one accepts the first, but the second resembles it so closely that we are irritated into feeling that not only the characters but we, too, are being manipulated. With the boys of the town the lieutenant finds himself moved by feelings he does not understand: "He wanted to begin the world again with them in a desert . . . [He] put out his hand in a gesture of affection—a touch, he didn't know what to do with it." To the villagers he is interrogating soon afterwards he says:

> "In my eyes—can't you understand—you are worth far more than he is. I want to give you"—he made a gesture with his hands which was valueless, because no one saw him—"everything."

Mr. Fellows is beefy, stupid, muddled; his wife a bourgeoise driven neurotic by the strain of exile:

> He was powerless and furious; he said, "You see what a hole you've put us in." He stumped back into the house and into his bedroom, roaming aimlessly among the boot-trees. Mrs. Fellows slept uneasily, dreaming of weddings. Once she said aloud, "My train. Be careful of my train."

A passage like this is surely cartoon-art; "dreaming of weddings" belongs to the same stylized regions as the huge mothers-in-law of the picture postcards, and "roaming among the boot-trees" is near-Thurberesque fantasy (how many boot-trees were there? were they larger than life? was there a seal behind each of them?).

The characters are being constantly pushed around, put into positions which are more effective for the pattern than probable; for example, the half-caste finally betraying the priest to the soldiers, simply saying "Father" from the clearing as the priest reaches the door of the hut—it is too obviously the Judas kiss. Or the priest's child sniggering evilly at him from among the refuse-heaps—the cracked vessel of the Truth facing the evidence of original sin; or the prison-companions who do not betray; or the boy who has admired the lieutenant and sensibly rejected the sickly tales of martyrdom, changing without warning when the priest has been executed, spitting at the lieutenant and opening the door for the new priest. Or the frequent, too appropriate, dreams. The priest sleeps, with guilt on his soul at the thought of his child:

> His eyes closed and immediately he began to dream. He was being pursued: he stood outside a door banging on it, begging for admission, but nobody answered—there was a word, a password, which would save him, but he had forgotten it. He tried desperately at random—cheese and child, California, excellency, milk, Vera Cruz. His feet had gone to sleep and he knelt outside the door. Then he knew why he wanted to get in: he wasn't being pursued at all: that was a mistake. His child lay beside him bleeding to death and this was a doctor's house. He banged on the door and shouted, "Even if I can't think of the right word, haven't you a heart?" The child was dying and looked up at him with middle-aged complacent wisdom. She said, "You animal," and he woke again crying.

The lieutenant should be happy now that he has finally caught the enemy of the new perfectionism, but is only lost and miserable:

> He went into the office: the pictures of the priest and the gunman were still pinned up on the wall: he tore them down—they would never be wanted again. Then he sat at his desk and put his head upon his hands and fell asleep with utter weariness. He couldn't remember afterwards anything of his dreams except laughter, laughter all the time, and a long passage in which he could find no door.

The dialogue is occasionally made to fit in the same way, as in the scene—brilliant as what it aims at being—in which the priest's illicit wine and brandy are drunk by the corrupt official and his hangers-on. The dialogue is trimmed to give a despondent, dribbling effect, e.g. the repeated "salud" as the precious drink disappears:

> "Is this the only bottle?" The man in drill watched him with frigid anxiety.
> "I'm afraid the only bottle."
> "Salud!"
> "And what," the Governor's cousin said, "were we talking about?"
> "About the first thing you could remember," the beggar said.
> "The first thing I can remember," the Jefe began with deliberation, "but this gentleman is not drinking."
> "I will have a little brandy."

"Salud!"

"Salud!"

"The first thing I can remember with any distinctness is my first communion. Ah, the thrill of the soul, my parents round me. . . ."

"How many parents then have you got?"

"Two, of course."

"They could not have been around you—you would have needed at least four—ha, ha."

"Salud!"

"Salud!"

And so on till all the drink has gone, and the priest is in tears. The scene lives in its dialogue, which has been formalized to the ends of the dramatic situation.

One's uneasiness increases as these kinds of detail pile up. It all finally confirms the impression of management from outside, of a lack of submission from within to the difficult and subtle matter of characterization.

"Immense readability," the reviewers say, and they are right; considerable immediate power from skilled overforcing of style, structure and character, and from a refusal to allow half-tones, uncertainties, complexities. I do not mean to imply that Greene deliberately aims at being "readable" in the popular sense, that he aims at commercial success. It seems more likely that both the distortion and the excessive control are results of Greene's view of life. This view is so insistent that it leads him consistently to falsify his fictional life. It has prevented him from producing, up to the present (though in *The End of the Affair* he was clearly disciplining both his structural and stylistic habits), a novel whose life we can "entertain as a possibility" whilst we are reading. But we continue to find his novels interesting simply because of the power of the view of life behind them, that very power which is causing the over-manipulation. We do not find experience convincingly recreated; we know all the time that we are in the presence of an unusually controlled allegory, a "show," to use Gerontion's word. The characters, I suggested, have a kind of life, but that life is always breathed into them by Greene's breath. The novels as a whole have a kind of life, but not the life of, say, *The Possessed,* in which we forget Dostoevsky and explore the revolutionary mentality. In Greene's novels we do not "explore experience"; we meet

Graham Greene. We enter continual reservations about what is
being done to experience, but we find the novels up to a point
arresting because they are forceful, melodramatic presentations of
an obsessed and imaginative personality.

There may well be a further, and more curious, reason for the
attraction of Greene's novels, one arising specifically from the fact
that they treat of religion. Greene presents us with a view of the
relationship between God and man in which the emphasis is almost entirely on the more dramatic aspects; the "who sweeps a
room as for thy sake" element is altogether lacking: "It was like a
short cut to the dark and magical heart of the faith . . . to the
night when the graves opened and the dead walked." This is only
one aspect of religious belief, and to think it all is to have an
inadequate view of religion. (I am concerned now, not with
Greene's aims but with what may be the attitudes of those who read
him.) It may be that exactly here lies an important part of the
appeal of these novels. The audience for them is primarily one
of unbelievers. To some unbelievers, I think, the more conservative, communal city-building features of faith are of little interest;
if they were to become religious, they wouldn't go in for it half-
way; they like their hellfire neat; they "drink damnation down like
brandy," to invert one of Greene's similes. The sort of excitement
they derive from these books may therefore be, curiously enough,
of the same order as that they find in the more "existentialist"
novels. Greene's kind of religion may be found interesting where
the less melodramatic poetry of religion would be found dull. Consciously, these readers may think they inhabit a reasonable, ordered
universe: but perhaps their taste in fiction betrays a subconscious
unease.

The Heresy of Our Time

by W. H. Auden

In its form, Graham Greene's novel, *The Ministry of Fear* (1943), is a thriller like John Buchan's *Thirty-nine Steps*. The thriller resembles the epic in that its subject is a war between two sides, but there are two important differences. First, the war is a secret undercover struggle. The outsider sees only peace and there are no visible distinguishing marks to show who is friend and who is foe. Second, the reader is made a partisan of one side. In the *Iliad,* even though it is written by Greeks, the Trojans are depicted as equally noble but in a thriller *They,* the enemy, are always bad.

The secrecy is an added excitement, but the partisanship is apt to make the thriller a bit priggish.

As Graham Greene himself says, "none of the books of adventure one read as a boy had an unhappy ending. And none of them was disturbed by a sense of pity for the beaten side."

Graham Greene succeeds, I think, in avoiding this crudity without sacrificing the drama, by relating the thriller to another literary form, the allegory. His thrillers are projected into outer melodramatic action of the struggles which go on unendingly in every mind and heart. Maybe this is why we like reading thrillers because each of us is a creature at war with himself. Further he is a self-deceptive creature who thinks he is feeling one thing or acting from one motive when his real feeling and motive are quite different.

There is, therefore, not a good side and a bad, nevertheless it does matter who wins. Again victory does not finally solve anything. A dangerous attack has been defeated, perhaps we understand ourselves a little better: that is all. A future, as difficult as before, perhaps more so, still remains.

"The Heresy of Our Time," by W. H. Auden. From *Renascence,* 1 (Spring 1949), 23–24. Copyright © 1949 by *Renascence.* Reprinted by permission of *Renascence.*

Graham Greene, then, employs a distinctive form: he also exhibits a distinctive concern. Just as Balzac came back again to avarice and Stendhal to ambition, so, in book after book, Graham Greene analyses the vice of pity, that corrupt parody of love and compassion which is so insidious and deadly for sensitive natures.

The secret war in *The Ministry of Fear* is between those who pity and those who can bear pain—other people's pain endlessly, the people who don't care. Yet both sides have a common bond; both have murdered. Arthur Rowe, the hero, has killed his wife to save her suffering from an incurable illness. Through his encounters with Hilfe, the Fascist agent, he is brought to realize that "it was her endurance and her patience which he had found most unbearable. He was trying to escape his own pain, not hers."

Behind pity for another lies self-pity, and behind self-pity lies cruelty.

To feel compassion for someone is to make oneself their equal; to pity them is to regard oneself as their superior and from that eminence the step to the torture chamber and the corrective labour camp is shorter than one thinks.

For providing us with such exciting reading and at the same time exposing so clearly a great and typical heresy of our time, Graham Greene deserves our lasting gratitude.

Felix Culpa?

by Evelyn Waugh

Of Mr. Graham Greene alone among contemporary writers one can say without affectation that his breaking silence with a new serious novel is a literary "event." It is eight years since the publication of "The Power and the Glory." During that time he has remained inconspicuous and his reputation has grown huge. We have had leisure to re-read his earlier books and to appreciate the gravity and intensity which underlie their severe modern surface. More than this, the spirit of the time has begun to catch up with them.

The artist, however aloof he holds himself, is always and specially the creature of the *zeitgeist;* however formally antique his tastes, he is in spite of himself in the advance guard. Men of affairs stumble far behind.

In the last twenty-five years the artist's interest has moved from sociology to eschatology. Out of hearing, out of sight, politicians and journalists and popular preachers exhort him to sing the splendours of high wages and sanitation. His eyes are on the Four Last Things, and so mountainous are the disappointments of recent history that there are already signs of a popular breakaway to join him, of a stampede to the heights.

I find the question most commonly asked by the agnostic is not: "Do you believe in the authenticity of the Holy House at Loreto?" or "Do you think an individual can justly inherit a right to the labour of another?" but "Do you believe in Hell?"

Mr. Greene has long shown an absorbing curiosity in the subject. In "Brighton Rock" he ingeniously gave life to a theological abstraction. We are often told: "The Church does not teach that any

"Felix Culpa?" by Evelyn Waugh. From *The Tablet,* 191 (June 5, 1948). Reprinted in *Commonweal,* 48 (July 16, 1948). Copyright © 1948 by *Commonweal.* Reprinted by permission of *The Tablet* and *Commonweal.*

man is damned. We only know that Hell exists for those who deserve it. Perhaps it is now empty and will remain so for all eternity." This was not the sentiment of earlier and healthier ages. The Last Judgment above the medieval door showed the lost and the saved as fairly equally divided; the path to salvation as exceedingly narrow and beset with booby-traps; the reek of brimstone was everywhere. Mr. Greene challenged the soft modern mood by creating a completely damnable youth. Pinkie of "Brighton Rock" is the ideal examinee for entry to Hell. He gets a pure alpha on every paper. His story is a brilliant and appalling imaginative achievement but falls short of the real hell-fire sermon by its very completeness. We leave our seats edified but smug. However vile we are, we are better than Pinkie. The warning of the preacher was that one unrepented slip obliterated the accumulated merits of a lifetime's struggle to be good. "Brighton Rock" might be taken to mean that one has to be as wicked as Pinkie before one runs into serious danger.

Mr. Greene's latest book, "The Heart of the Matter," should be read as the complement of "Brighton Rock." It poses a vastly more subtle problem. Its hero speaks of the Church as "knowing all the answers," but his life and death comprise a problem to which the answer is in the mind of God alone, the reconciliation of perfect justice with perfect mercy. It is a book which only a Catholic could write and only a Catholic can understand. I mean that only a Catholic can understand the nature of the problem. Many Catholics, I am sure, will gravely misunderstand it, particularly in the United States of America, where its selection as the Book of the Month will bring it to a much larger public than can profitably read it. There are loyal Catholics here and in America who think it the function of the Catholic writer to produce only advertising brochures setting out in attractive terms the advantages of Church membership. To them this profoundly reverent book will seem a scandal. For it not only portrays Catholics as unlikeable human beings but shows them as tortured by their Faith. It will be the object of controversy and perhaps even of condemnation. Thousands of heathen will read it with innocent excitement, quite unaware that they are intruding among the innermost mysteries of faith. There is a third class who will see what this book intends and yet be troubled by doubt of its theological propriety.

Mr. Greene divides his fiction into "Novels" and "Entertainments." Superficially there is no great difference between the two categories. There is no Ruth Draper switch from comic to pathetic. "Novels" and "Entertainments" are both written in the same grim style, both deal mainly with charmless characters, both have a structure of sound, exciting plot. You cannot tell from the skeleton whether the man was baptized or not. And that is the difference; the "Novels" have been baptized, held deep under in the waters of life. The author has said: "These characters are not my creation but God's. They have an eternal destiny. They are not merely playing a part for the reader's amusement. They are souls whom Christ died to save." This, I think, explains his preoccupation with the charmless. The children of Adam are not a race of noble savages who need only a divine spark to perfect them. They are aboriginally corrupt. Their tiny relative advantages of intelligence and taste and good looks and good manners are quite insignificant. The compassion and condescension of the Word becoming flesh are glorified in the depths.

As I have said above, the style of writing is grim. It is not a specifically literary style at all. The words are functional, devoid of sensuous attraction, of ancestry and of independent life. Literary stylists regard language as intrinsically precious and its proper use as a worthy and pleasant task. A polyglot could read Mr. Greene, lay him aside, retain a sharp memory of all he said and yet, I think, entirely forget what tongue he was using. The words are simply mathematical signs for his thought. Moreover, no relation is established between writer and reader. The reader has not had a conversation with a third party such as he enjoys with Sterne or Thackeray. Nor is there within the structure of the story an observer through whom the events are recorded and the emotions transmitted. It is as though, out of an infinite length of film, sequences had been cut which, assembled, comprise an experience which is the reader's alone, without any correspondence to the experience of the protagonists. The writer has become director and producer. Indeed, the affinity to the film is everywhere apparent. It is the camera's eye which moves from the hotel balcony to the street below, picks out the policeman, follows him to his office, moves about the room from the handcuffs on the wall to the broken rosary in the drawer, recording significant detail. It is the modern way of telling a story. In Elizabethan drama one can usually discern an artistic sense formed on the dumb-show and the masque. In Henry James's novels scene after scene evolves as though on the stage of a drawing-room comedy. Now it is the cinema which has taught a new habit of narrative. Perhaps it is the only contribution the cinema is destined to make to the arts.

There is no technical trick about good story-telling in this or any other manner. All depends on the natural qualities of the narrator's mind, whether or no he sees events in a necessary sequence. Mr. Greene is a story-teller of genius. Born in another age, he would still be spinning yarns. His particular habits are accidental. The plot of "The Heart of the Matter" might well have been used by M. Simenon or Mr. Somerset Maugham.

The scene is a West African port in war time. It has affinities with the Brighton of "Brighton Rock," parasitic, cosmopolitan, corrupt. The population are all strangers, British officials, detribalized natives, immigrant West Indian Negroes, Asiatics, Syrians. There are poisonous gossip at the club and voodoo bottles on the wharf, intrigues for administrative posts, intrigues to monopolize the illicit diamond trade. The hero, Scobie, is deputy-commissioner of police, one of the oldest inhabitants among the white officials; he has a compassionate liking for the place and the people. He is honest and unpopular and, when the story begins, he has been passed over for promotion. His wife Louise is also unpopular, for other reasons. She is neurotic and pretentious. Their only child died at school in England. Both are Catholic. His failure to get made commissioner is the final humiliation. She whines and nags to escape to South Africa. Two hundred pounds are needed to send her. Husband and wife are found together in the depths of distress.

The illegal export of diamonds is prevalent, both as industrial stones for the benefit of the enemy and gems for private investment. Scobie's police are entirely ineffective in stopping it, although it is notorious that two Syrians, Tallit and Yusef, are competitors for the monopoly. A police-spy is sent from England to investigate. He falls in love with Louise. Scobie, in order to fulfil his promise to get Louise out of the country, borrows money from Yusef. As a result of this association he is involved in an attempt to "frame" Tallit. The police-spy animated by hate and jealousy is on his heels. Meanwhile survivors from a torpedoed ship are brought across from French territory, among them an English bride widowed in the sinking. She and Scobie fall in love and she becomes his mistress. Yusef secures evidence of the intrigue and blackmails Scobie into definitely criminal participation in his trade. His association with Yusef culminates in the murder of Ali, Scobie's supposedly devoted native servant, whom he now suspects of giving information to the police-spy. Louise returns. Unable to abandon either woman, inextricably involved in crime, hunted by his enemy, Scobie takes poison; his women become listlessly acquiescent to other suitors.

These are the bare bones of the story, the ground plan on which almost any kind of building might be erected. The art of story-telling has little to do with the choice of plot. One can imagine the dreariest kind of film—(Miss Bacall's pretty head lolling on the stretcher)—accurately constructed to these specifications. Mr. Greene, as his admirers would expect, makes of his material a precise and plausible drama. His technical mastery has never been better manifested than in his statement of the scene—the sweat and infection, the ill-built town which is beautiful for a few minutes at sundown, the brothel where all men are equal, the vultures, the priest who, when he laughed "swung his great empty-sounding bell to and fro, Ho ho, ho, like a leper proclaiming his misery," the snobbery of the second-class public schools, the law which all can evade, the ever-present haunting underworld of gossip, spying, bribery, violence and betrayal. There are incidents of the highest imaginative power—Scobie at the bedside of a dying child, improvising his tale of the Bantus. It is so well done that one forgets the doer. The characters are real people whose moral and spiritual predicament is our own because they are part of our personal experience.

As I have suggested above, Scobie is the complement of Pinkie. Both believe in damnation and believe themselves damned. Both die in mortal sin as defined by moral theologians. The conclusion of the book is the reflection that no one knows the secrets of the human heart or the nature of God's mercy. It is improper to speculate on another's damnation. Nevertheless the reader is haunted by the question: Is Scobie damned? One does not really worry very much about whether Becky Sharp or Fagin is damned. It is the

central question of "The Heart of the Matter." I believe that Mr.
Greene thinks him a saint. Perhaps I am wrong in this, but in any
case Mr. Greene's opinion on that matter is of no more value
than the reader's. Scobie is not Mr. Greene's creature, devised to
illustrate a thesis. He is a man of independent soul. Can one separate his moral from his spiritual state? Both are complex and
ambiguous.

First, there is his professional delinquency. In the first pages he
appears as an Aristides, disliked for his rectitude; by the end of
the book he has become a criminal. There is nothing inevitable in
his decline. He compromises himself first in order to get his wife's
passage money. She is in a deplorable nervous condition; perhaps,
even, her reason is in danger. He is full of compassion. But she is
making his own life intolerable; he wants her out of the way for
his own peace. As things turn out the trip to South Africa was quite
unnecessary. Providence had its own cure ready if he had only
waited. He gets the commissionership in the end, which was ostensibly all that Louise wanted. But behind that again lies the deeper
cause of her melancholy, that Scobie no longer loves her in the way
that would gratify her vanity. And behind the betrayal of his official trust lies the futility of his official position. The law he ad-
ministers has little connection with morals or justice. It is all a matter of regulations—a Portuguese sea-captain's right to correspond
with his daughter in Germany, the right of a tenant to divide and
sub-let her hut, the right of a merchant to provide out of his own
property for the security of his family. He knows that his sub-
ordinates are corrupt and can do nothing about it. Whom or what
has he in fact betrayed, except his own pride?

Secondly, there is his adultery. His affection for the waif cast
up on the beach is at first compassionate and protective; it becomes
carnal. Why? He is an elderly man long schooled in chastity. There
is another suitor of Helen Rolt, Bagster the Air Force philanderer.
It is Bagster's prowling round the bungalow which precipitates
the change of relationship. It is Bagster in the background who
makes him persevere in adultery when his wife's return affords a
convenient occasion for parting. Bagster is a promiscuous cad.
Helen must be saved from Bagster. Why? Scobie arrogates to himself the prerogations of providence. He presumes that an illicit
relation with himself is better than an illicit relation with Bagster.

But why, in fact, need it have been illicit? She might marry Bagster.

Thirdly there is the murder of Ali. We do not know whether Ali was betraying him. If he had not been a smuggler and an adulterer there would have been nothing to betray. Ali dies to emphasize the culpability of these sins.

Fourthly there are the sacrilegious communions which Louise forces upon him; and fifthly, his suicide, a re-statement of that blasphemy in other terms. He dies believing himself damned but also in an obscure way—at least in a way that is obscure to me— believing that he is offering his damnation as a loving sacrifice for others.

We are told that he is actuated throughout by the love of God. A love, it is true that falls short of trust, but a love, we must suppose, which sanctifies his sins. That is the heart of the matter. Is such a sacrifice feasible? To me the idea is totally unintelligible, but it is not unfamiliar. Did the Quietists not speak in something like these terms? I ask in all humility whether nowadays logical rule-of-thumb Catholics are not a little too humble towards the mystics. We are inclined to say: "Ah, that is mysticism. I'm quite out of my depth there," as though the subject were higher mathematics, while in fact our whole Faith is essentially mystical. We may well fight shy of discussing ecstatic states of prayer with which we have no acquaintance, but sacrilege and suicide are acts of which we are perfectly capable. To me the idea of willing my own damnation for the love of God is either a very loose poetical expression or a mad blasphemy, for the God who accepted that sacrifice could be neither just nor lovable.

Mr. Greene has put a quotation from Péguy at the beginning of the book *"Le pécheur est au coeur même de chrétienté . . . Nul n'est aussi compétent que le pécheur en matière de chrétienté. Nul, si ce n'est le saint,"* and it seems to me probable that it was in his mind to illustrate the *"Nouveau Théologien"* from which it is taken, just as in "Brighton Rock" he illustrates the Penny Catechism. The theme of that remarkable essay is that Christianity is a city to which a bad citizen belongs and the good stranger does not. Péguy describes the Church, very beautifully, as a chain of saints and sinners with clasped fingers, pulling one another up to Jesus.

But there are also passages which, if read literally, are grossly exorbitant. Péguy was not three years a convert when he wrote it, and
he was not in communion with the Church. He daily saw men and
women, who seemed to him lacking his own intense spirituality,
trooping up to the altar rails while he was obliged to stay in his
place excommunicate. The *"Nouveau Théologien"* is his meditation
on his predicament. He feels there is a city of which he is a true
citizen, but it is not the community of conventional practicing
Catholics, who are not, in his odd, often repeated phrase, *"compétent en matière de chrétienté."* He feels a kinship with the saints
that these conventional church-goers do not know and in his
strange, narrow, brooding mind he makes the preposterous deduc-
tion that this very true and strong bond is made, not by his faith
and love, but by his sins. *"Littéralement,"* he writes, *"celui qui est
pécheur, celui qui commet un péché est déjà chrétien, est en cela
même chrétien. On pourrait presque dire est un bon chrétien."*
"Littéralement"?: what is the precise force of that passage? Much
depends on it. Does "literally" mean that any and every sinner is
by virtue of his sin a Christian? Was Yusef a sinner and therefore
Christian? No, because Péguy has already stated that strangers
outside the chain of clasped hands cannot commit sin at all. Is
Yusef damned? Can a sinner by this definition never be damned?
The argument works in a circle of undefined terms. And what of
the *"presque"*? How does one "almost" say something? Is one prevented by the fear of shocking others or the realization at the last
moment that what one was going to say does not in fact make
sense? In that case why record it? Why "almost" say it? This is not
a matter of quibbling. If Péguy is saying anything at all, he is
saying something very startling and something which people seem
to find increasingly important. Mr. Greene has removed the argument from Péguy's mumbled version and re-stated it in brilliantly
plain human terms; and it is there, at the heart of the matter, that
the literary critic must resign his judgment to the theologian.

A Postscript to Evelyn Waugh

by Canon Joseph Cartmell

Mr. Evelyn Waugh's comments on the theology of this book are, in my view, unimpeachable. Fr. Rank, to console the widow, expressed his opinion that Scobie really loved God. He could hardly mean it in the literal sense, unless he was assuming that Scobie's sins were indeliberate, the voluntary acts of a warped mind —an assumption which is against the whole tenor of the book. Scobie is a deliberate sinner up to and including the taking of the poison. Whether he was damned is another question, to which we do not know the answer. His attempt to make an act of contrition and then an act of charity when the poison was beginning to work may indicate repentance. We are not told and we do not know what transpired between God and him in his last moments. There is the old saying to check undue severity:

> *Betwixt the stirrup and the ground*
> *He mercy sought and mercy found.*

As the book depicts him, Scobie retained his Faith. He lost hope; his first deliberate mortal sin forfeited charity. He intensified the forfeiture by piling sin on sin; and, by losing hope, he lost the will to repent. He was offered many actual graces leading to repentance; these he rejected. He remained therefore with what is technically known as dead Faith, for by charity is Faith alive. Being without charity, he could not really love God; for the real love of God, the love that is salutary, is the work of charity. All this is true up to the time of his taking the poison. What happened afterwards, as I said above, we can only guess.

"A Postscript to Evelyn Waugh" (published in *The Tablet* as "Canon Joseph Cartmell Writes"), by Canon Joseph Cartmell. Reprinted in *Commonweal*, 48 (July 16, 1948), 325–26. Copyright © 1948 by *Commonweal*. Reprinted by permission of *Commonweal*.

Making his first bad communion, he prayed: "O God, I offer up my damnation to you. Take it. Use it for them." I do not think that Mr. Greene means to assign any real value to this offering. You cannot do evil that good may come of it. Such an offering could have no worth with God. It is, as Mr. Waugh says, a mad blasphemy. Indeed, no positive good came of Scobie's death. Neither Louise Scobie nor Helen Rolt was morally uplifted by his act. The only good was a negative one, the removal of himself as a source of sin to them. Scobie was in fact a very bad moral coward. He could have escaped from his entanglement by a comparatively simple resolution. He would not take it. His attempt to give an air of moral respectability to his sins and his suicide, as though they were helping others, was, objectively, pure sham.

The study of Scobie is done with power. But I feel a weakness. No man can indeed appreciate to the full the idea of the eternal loss of God; but here one is left with the impression that Scobie is merely going into exile in the next world; in his heart he regrets to lose God, but, since he was always happiest when alone, he will not, in the long run, when he has got used to things in the beyond, be very unhappy; he will have the peace of the solitary. Briefly, in spite of his shrinking, he takes Hell very quietly. So it seems to me. I hope I am not misinterpreting Mr. Greene.

The Sanctified Sinner

by George Orwell

A fairly large proportion of the distinguished novels of the last few decades have been written by Catholics and have even been describable as Catholic novels. One reason for this is that the conflict not only between this world and the next world but between sanctity and goodness is a fruitful theme of which the ordinary, unbelieving writer cannot make use. Graham Greene used it once successfully, in *The Power and the Glory,* and once, with very much more doubtful success, in *Brighton Rock.* His latest book, *The Heart of the Matter,* is, to put it as politely as possible, not one of his best, and gives the impression of having been mechanically constructed, the familiar conflict being set out like an algebraic equation, with no attempt at psychological probability.

Here is the outline of the story: The time is 1942 and the place is a West African British colony, unnamed but probably the Gold Coast. A certain Major Scobie, Deputy Commissioner of Police and a Catholic convert, finds a letter bearing a German address hidden in the cabin of the captain of a Portuguese ship. The letter turns out to be a private one and completely harmless, but it is, of course, Scobie's duty to hand it over to higher authority. However, the pity he feels for the Portuguese captain is too much for him, and he destroys the letter and says nothing about it. Scobie, it is explained to us, is a man of almost excessive conscientiousness. He does not drink, takes bribes, keep Negro mistresses, or indulge in bureaucratic intrigue, and he is, in fact, disliked on all sides because of his uprightness, like Aristides the Just. His leniency toward the

Portuguese captain is his first lapse. After it, his life becomes a sort of fable on the theme of "Oh, what a tangled web we weave," and in every single instance it is the goodness of his heart that leads him astray. Actuated at the start by pity, he has a love affair with a girl who has been rescued from a torpedoed ship. He continues with the affair largely out of a sense of duty, since the girl will go to pieces morally if abandoned; he also lies about her to his wife, so as to spare her the pangs of jealousy. Since he intends to persist in his adultery, he does not go to confession, and in order to lull his wife's suspicions he tells her that he has gone. This involves him in the truly fearful act of taking the Sacrament while in a state of mortal sin. By this time, there are other complications, all caused in the same manner, and Scobie finally decides that the only way out is through the unforgivable sin of suicide. Nobody else must be allowed to suffer through his death; it will be so arranged as to look like an accident. As it happens, he bungles one detail, and the fact that he has committed suicide becomes known. The book ends with a Catholic priest's hinting, with doubtful orthodoxy, that Scobie is perhaps not damned. Scobie, however, had not entertained any such hope. White all through, with a stiff upper lip, he had gone to what he believed to be certain damnation out of pure gentlemanliness.

I have not parodied the plot of the book. Even when dressed up in realistic details, it is just as ridiculous as I have indicated. The thing most obviously wrong with it is that Scobie's motives, assuming one could believe in them, do not adequately explain his actions. Another question that comes up is: Why should this novel have its setting in West Africa? Except that one of the characters is a Syrian trader, the whole thing might as well be happening in a London suburb. The Africans exist only as an occasionally mentioned background, and the thing that would actually be in Scobie's mind the whole time—the hostility between black and white, and the struggle against the local nationalist movement—is not mentioned at all. Indeed, although we are shown his thoughts in considerable detail, he seldom appears to think about his work, and then only of trivial aspects of it, and never about the war, although the date is 1942. All he is interested in is his own progress toward damnation. The improbability of this shows up against the colonial setting, but it is an improbability that is present in *Brighton*

Rock as well, and that is bound to result from foisting theological preoccupations upon simple people anywhere.

The central idea of the book is that it is better, spiritually higher, to be an erring Catholic than a virtuous pagan. Graham Greene would probably subscribe to the statement of Maritain, made apropos of Léon Bloy, that "there is but one sadness—not to be a saint." A saying of Péguy's is quoted on the title page of the book to the effect that the sinner is "at the very heart of Christianity" and knows more of Christianity than anyone else does, except the saint. All such sayings contain, or can be made to contain, the fairly sinister suggestion that ordinary human decency is of no value and that any one sin is no worse than any other sin. In addition, it is impossible not to feel a sort of snobbishness in Mr. Greene's attitude, both here and in his other books written from an explicitly Catholic standpoint. He appears to share the idea, which has been floating around ever since Baudelaire, that there is something rather *distingué* in being damned; Hell is a sort of high-class night club, entry to which is reserved for Catholics only, since the others, the non-Catholics, are too ignorant to be held guilty, like the beasts that perish. We are carefully informed that Catholics are no better than anybody else; they even, perhaps, have a tendency to be worse, since their temptations are greater. In modern Catholic novels, in both France and England, it is, indeed, the fashion to include bad priests, or at least inadequate priests, as a change from Father Brown. (I imagine that one major objective of young English Catholic writers is not to resemble Chesterton.) But all the while— drunken, lecherous, criminal, or damned outright—the Catholics retain their superiority since they alone know the meaning of good and evil. Incidentally, it is assumed in *The Heart of the Matter,* and in most of Mr. Greene's other books, that no one outside the Catholic Church has the most elementary knowledge of Christian doctrine.

This cult of the sanctified sinner seems to me to be frivolous, and underneath it there probably lies a weakening of belief, for when people really believed in Hell, they were not so fond of striking graceful attitudes on its brink. More to the point, by trying to clothe theological speculations in flesh and blood, it produces psychological absurdities. In *The Power and the Glory,* the struggle between this-worldly and other-worldly values is convincing because it is not occurring inside one person. On the one side, there is the priest, a poor creature in some ways but made heroic by his belief in his own thaumaturgic powers; on the other side, there is the lieutenant, representing human justice and material progress, and also a heroic figure after his fashion. They can respect each other, perhaps, but not understand each other. The priest, at any rate, is not credited with any very complex thoughts. In *Brighton Rock,* on the other hand, the central situation is incredible, since it presupposes that the most brutishly stupid person can, merely by having been brought up a Catholic, be capable of great intellectual subtlety. Pinkie, the race-course gangster, is a species of satanist, while his still more limited girl friend understands and even states the difference between the categories "right and wrong" and "good and evil." In, for example, Mauriac's *Thérèse* sequence, the spiritual conflict does not outrage probability, because it is not pretended that Thérèse is a normal person. She is a chosen spirit, pursuing her salvation over a long period and by a difficult route, like a patient stretched out on the psychiatrist's sofa. To take an opposite instance, Evelyn Waugh's *Brideshead Revisited,* in spite of improbabilities, which are traceable partly to the book's being written in the first person, succeeds because the situation is itself a normal one. The Catholic characters bump up against problems they would meet with in real life; they do not suddenly move on to a different intellectual plane as soon as their religious beliefs are involved. Scobie is incredible because the two halves of him do not fit together. If he were capable of getting into the kind of mess that is described, he would have got into it years earlier. If he really felt that adultery was mortal sin, he would stop committing it; if he persisted in it, his sense of sin would weaken. If he believed in Hell, he would not risk going there merely to spare the feelings of a couple of neurotic women. And one might add that if he were the kind of man we are told he is—that is, a man whose chief characteristic is a horror of causing pain—he would not be an officer in a colonial police force.

There are other improbabilities, some of which arise out of Mr. Greene's method of handling a love affair. Every novelist has his own conventions, and, just as in an E. M. Forster novel there is a strong tendency for the characters to die suddenly without sufficient cause, so in a Graham Greene novel there is a tendency for people

to go to bed together almost at sight and with no apparent pleasure
to either party. Often this is credible enough, but in *The Heart of
the Matter* its effect is to weaken a motive that, for the purposes of
the story, ought to be a very strong one. Again, there is the usual,
perhaps unavoidable, mistake of making everyone too highbrow.
It is not only that Major Scobie is a theologian. His wife, who is
represented as an almost complete fool, reads poetry, while the
detective who is sent by the Field Security Corps to spy on Scobie
even writes poetry. Here one is up against the fact that it is not easy
for most modern writers to imagine the mental processes of anyone
who is not a writer.

It seems a pity, when one remembers how admirably he has written of Africa elsewhere, that Mr. Greene should have made just
this book out of his war-time African experiences. The fact that the
book is set in Africa while the action takes place almost entirely
inside a tiny white community gives it an air of triviality. However,
one must not carp too much. It is pleasant to see Mr. Greene starting up again after so long a silence, and in post-war England it is
a remarkable feat for a novelist to write a novel at all. At any
rate, Mr. Greene has not been permanently demoralised by the
habits acquired during the war, like so many others. But one may
hope that his next book will have a different theme, or, if not, that
he will at least remember that a perception of the vanity of earthly
things, though it may be enough to get one into Heaven, is not
sufficient equipment for the writing of a novel.

The End of the Affair

by Ian Gregor

Of all Graham Greene's novels *The End of the Affair* is most likely to get summary justice. The reason lies, quite simply, in the apparent directness and explicitness with which the religious theme has been presented. In consequence, literary criticism tends to melt much too rapidly in the heat of extra-literary convictions.

For the reader who shares Greene's religious views, the theological contentions in *The End of the Affair* will tend to loom too large in his perspective. He may, for instance, welcome the novel as an intelligent and sensitive discussion of problems which are of great importance to him and be pleased that these questions are being given such persuasive publicity. Another kind of Catholic reader may be irritated precisely by the fact that publicity is being given to views which he considers, if not actually heretical, at least severely mistaken in emphasis. Both readers are guilty of the same confusion of thought. They fail to distinguish between theology and theology-in-fiction, between "views" and "the use of views" as artistic material. For both readers this failure has its consolation. If orthodoxy in fiction is unlikely to make for religious conversions, heterodoxy, similarly presented, is unlikely to disturb the faith of the believer. The influence of fiction is more elusive than the believer tends to think, though it would be rash to assume that it is less penetrating.

The reader who does not share the religious views behind *The End of the Affair* will tend to depreciate their significance. He will see them perhaps as a gratuitous addition to an otherwise satisfactory work; he will argue that the novel is finally "closed" to him

"The End of the Affair," by Ian Gregor. From *The Moral and the Story*, by Ian Gregor and Brian Nicholas (London: Faber & Faber, Ltd., 1962), pp. 192–206. Copyright © 1962 by Ian Gregor and Brian Nicholas. Reprinted by permission of the publisher.

because he finds it philosophically or theologically unacceptable; he may go further and argue that the introduction of the divine into imaginative literature is an unwarrantable extension of the province of art. In doing so, he would forget Dante, Marlowe and Dostoevsky. He would forget, too, that however alien the miraculous is to his own thought and experience, it has clearly not been alien to a great number of the human race; and there certainly seems no intrinsic reason why such experience, genuinely felt, should be prohibited from art. Again there is the basic failure to distinguish between theology and theology-in-fiction. Where a certain kind of Catholic reader sees in Greene an apologia for his faith, a certain kind of sceptic sees an indictment of his. But fortunately Greene has written a novel and not a theological discourse, and it is this which makes the hypothetical reactions I have been describing largely irrelevant, and allows the whole matter to be taken further.

When this has been said it is no less important to stress that relevant discussion of *The End of the Affair* does not imply that the critic "drops" his beliefs. This charade would be as undesirable as it would be unnecessary. Rather we have to find a way of talking about a religious novel which does not rely for its cogency upon our own beliefs, not because these should be neutralized, but because they should hardly be brought into play. There is a sense in which *all* discussion is eventually theological or philosophical, but clearly this does not render invalid the discussion which leads us to that terminus. Literary criticism, in so far as it remains that, only takes place between intermediate stations.

We can begin by setting down briefly the plot of *The End of the Affair*:

> Bendrix, a middle-aged novelist, and Sarah, the wife of a Senior Civil Servant, are lovers. Their "affair," lasting through most of the war, runs an uneven, passionate and unscrupulous course, largely owing to the tormented jealousy and bitterness of Bendrix. It is brought to an abrupt end during an air raid. Bendrix is knocked unconscious under a door. After a few minutes he recovers, goes upstairs, and finds Sarah on her knees praying. She leaves the house and he doesn't see her again. All his attempts to get in contact with her fail. Eighteen months later Bendrix accidentally meets Sarah's husband, Henry. He invites Bendrix for a drink, and tells

him that he is worried by Sarah's frequent absences from home.
He is thinking of engaging a private inquiry agent. Bendrix urges
Henry to allow him to make the engagement. Unknown to Henry
he does so, and proceeds to get reports on Sarah's movements and
to obtain her private journal. Reading the journal he learns that
during the air raid, Sarah, believing Bendrix to be dead, had made
a bargain with God promising that she would give Bendrix up if
He would restore him to life. She tries, in vain, various ways of
forgetting him. She visits a rationalist preacher, hoping that he will
convince her to break her bargain. But his arguments only feed her
faith. Her love for Bendrix continues as strongly as ever, and, in
the closing entries of her journal, she begs God for peace. Deeply
moved by this account Bendrix attempts to see her, but she avoids
him, even going out into the rain although she is unwell. A week
goes by, and then Bendrix receives a telephone call from Henry to
say that Sarah is dead. After her death, and through her intervention, the private detective's little boy is cured of appendicitis and
the rationalist preacher of a strawberry mark. Invited by Henry,
Bendrix goes to share his house, his jealousy and hatred of Sarah's
lover unabated by the fact that his rival was not human but divine.

This bald recital of events is more than usually inadequate because the novel is told from the point of view of Bendrix, whose
bitter and distorted view of events gives an extraordinary impression of emotional immediacy; it also makes it difficult for the reader
to assess them objectively. This problem, of course, always arises
when the narrator's point of view and the author's are not identified.

Allowing for this, however, we might—given this summary of
the plot—presume that this was a novel, basically, about adultery
and remorse. Whatever else Sarah is, she is a "fallen woman"; on
that state of moral guilt she turns her back with extraordinary
determination and agony of mind, and returns to her husband.
Greene, we might go on to conclude, has provided us in this novel
with an endorsement of Hardy's contention in *Tess of the D'Urber-
villes*: "Who was the moral woman? The beauty and ugliness of
a character lay not only in its achievements, but in its aims and
impulses; its true history lay not among things done, but among
things willed." If Sarah triumphs in anything it would seem precisely to be in her will to give up Bendrix. And thus the moral
order is affirmed and restored. All this would be a reasonable in-

ference from the account of the plot, but it plays false to our experiences of reading the novel.

The End of the Affair only has the appearance of a moral story, just as it has the appearance of a detective story. There is what looks like adultery and what looks like remorse. But these are false clues leading to a false conclusion, just as the detective by dusting the door bells tracks down Sarah's visits to the rationalist preacher and concludes the mystery is solved. "Adultery" and "remorse" like "the private detective" and "the unknown man" are stock-properties of a certain kind of plot which Greene takes over to explore a theme connected neither with morality nor detection. The theme is, quite simply, grace, and although it raises no moral problems for Bendrix or for Sarah, it certainly raises a critical one for the reader of the novel.

Always present in Greene's earlier religious novels, the problem of grace becomes fully explicit only with *The End of the Affair*. In *Brighton Rock* and *The Power and the Glory* Greene makes reference to the "appalling strangeness of the mercy of God"; in *The End of the Affair* it becomes his *subject*. The transition is crucial. The reader of the earlier novels takes in the reference to grace as a meaningful one, it indicates a direction which he is asked to observe rather than explore, in the manner of an arrow in the margin of a map indicating proximate places. In *The End of the Affair* the reader is presented with a different kind of map. The arrows are reversed in direction, pointing towards the central section which has been left blank. In one map the arrows serve to give a context to an area already defined; in the other they plot the limits of the known. With the central section blank, the relation of the other sections to each other becomes problematical. Whichever road we take we are confronted with the unknown. And the reason is not far to seek. At the centre of *The End of the Affair*, we have Christ present in the world, supernatural grace in the presence of the natural order, and to trace out this spiritual cartography one would need to be God. And if we should presume to speculate we have St. Paul's reminder, "How incomprehensible are His judgments, and how unsearchable His ways! For who hath known the mind of the Lord? Or who hath been His counsellor." M. Sartre has provided a gloss on this for the novelist: "In the sight of God, who penetrates through appearances without coming to a halt in them, there is no novel, no art, since art lives by appearance. God is not an artist. . . ." For the same reason He can never be directly included in a work of fiction, but in *The End of the Affair* the degree of directness is such as to make Him virtually a "character." If the purpose of art is to reveal an order in life, by imposing an order on it, God cannot be imposed on in this way. If this is the picture in general terms, we have to go on to ask what kind of effect this "unknowable," and necessarily unknowable, centre has on the actual working out of the novel.

"You seem to have a very strange set of values," Father Crompton remarks to Bendrix, and, though it is clear what he means, the same remark made to Sarah would be much more illuminating. Complex and tormented as he is, Bendrix is a natural inhabitant of a pagan, materialist world, sharing its values, its assumptions: "If two people loved, they slept together; it was a mathematical formula, tested and proved by 'human experience.' " It is a wholly characteristic remark of Bendrix, arrogant, sardonic, amoral. But Sarah's character defies this kind of summary. "She was good, Bendrix. People talk but she was good." Henry's remark is not at variance with the reader's experience, and yet, when we begin to ponder the nature of her "goodness," we wonder just why this should be so.

Consider the contrasting attitudes of Bendrix and Sarah towards "the affair" itself. Consumed with jealousy whenever Sarah is absent, the only happiness Bendrix knows is when he actually possesses her, and even then it is interrupted by accusation and bitterness. Sarah, looking back on the affair, observes: "We were sometimes so happy and never in our lives have we known more unhappiness. It's as if we were working together on the same statue, cutting it out of each other's misery." The misery proceeds, however, from different causes. In Bendrix's case it is because of the inherent precariousness of the whole affair; in Sarah's, it is Bendrix's own unhappiness which causes hers. She accepts the affair in a way that he never does and Bendrix gives us the reason: "She had no doubts. The moment only mattered. . . . I never lose the consciousness of time; to me, the present is never here . . . it is always last year or next week." We are meant to take this as indicating a special quality in Sarah, but it seems to me the point is ambiguously present. If there is generosity and trust in Sarah's immersion in the moment, there is also the reason why the affair never grows, never becomes a relationship, drawing on memory, confident in hope. And it is this that Bendrix is seeking, however blindly and selfishly. At the heart of Sarah's warmth there is something which Greene seeks to persuade us is divinity, but its features uncomfortably resemble inhumanity.

It is this tense ambiguity which serves to explain the odd note which sounds so often in Sarah and Bendrix's exchanges. We have it here, for instance:

> It angered me that she didn't make any claim. "You may be right. I'm only saying I want you to be happy. I hate your being unhappy. I don't mind anything you do that makes you happy."
>
> "You just want an excuse. If I sleep with somebody else you feel you can do the same—any time."
>
> "That's neither here nor there. I want you to be happy that's all."
>
> "You'd make my bed for me?"
>
> "Perhaps."

Here the tide appears to be moving strongly in one direction, but there is a powerful undercurrent moving against it. The overt intention is to show Sarah's virtually superhuman selflessness, but there is an undertone which reveals a curious amoral indifference. The altitude from which Greene's observation is made is so great that all the distinctive features are lost in the general blur.

The same thing happens, disastrously, in the scene where Henry, who is ill, has unwittingly interrupted Sarah and Bendrix's lovemaking. He leaves and Bendrix remarks to Sarah:

> "Do you mind?" She shook her head. I don't really know what I meant—I think I had an idea that the sight of Henry might have aroused remorse, but she had a wonderful way of eliminating remorse. Unlike the rest of us she was unhaunted by guilt. In her view when a thing was done, it was done: remorse died with the act. She would have thought it unreasonable of Henry, if he had caught us, to be angry for more than a moment. Catholics are always said to be freed in the confessional from the mortmain of the past—certainly in that respect you could have called her a born Catholic,

although she believed in God as little as I did. Or so I thought then
and wonder now.

The ambiguity of this is so considerable that it becomes ironic.
That it should become so suggests how far Greene is prepared to
go in establishing "virtue" independent of morality. The declared
intention of the passage would seem again to be that Sarah's love
is so complete and overwhelming that it obliterates all other considerations. But, if that is the surface of the passage, it covers
anomalies and confusions. It is left to Bendrix, the amoral seducer,
to raise the moral question, although he quickly realizes its irrelevance to Sarah. She had "a wonderful way of eliminating remorse,"
which is coming close to saying that she is without conscience. We
can see that a result of Sarah's "life in the moment" is that any
form of moral appraisal is rendered null and void; an act is simply
what it is, having neither history nor consequence. From this point
of view, "anger" on Henry's part at his wife's seduction is "unreasonable." The palpable unreality of this is such that we feel the
justice of Bendrix's earlier remark to Sarah, "you simply haven't
caught up yet on ordinary human emotions."

It is not always easy to distinguish Bendrix speaking from
Greene speaking through him and the reference to Catholics would
seem to be the latter. In that case it is difficult to understand the
misrepresentation. Only sorrow for sin can free Catholics from "the
mortmain of the past," and the confessional is there as a formal
means to this end. If it is Bendrix speaking in a tone of sardonic
criticism, then his perception of Sarah being "unhaunted by guilt,"
and her seeming to be "a born Catholic," loses considerably in
force. Whatever emerges from this confused and confusing passage,
one thing is clear, that the quality Greene is trying to isolate in
Sarah has not merely nothing to do with morality, but seems
actively opposed to it.

If the reason for these strange ambiguities and distortions is that
Greene is trying to mirror in human love the absolute selflessness
of the divine, what happens when the emphasis shifts and Sarah
addresses not Bendrix but God? Greene's purpose is to show us that
her love was all of a piece, whether the object was Bendrix or God.
A passage like this is carefully interchangeable:

She had no doubts. The moment only mattered. Eternity is said not to be an extension of time, but an absence of time, and sometimes it seemed to me that her abandonment touched that strange mathematical point of endlessness, a point with no width, occupying no space.

It is not difficult to convert that "point" of Bendrix's into God. And years later Bendrix reads a torn page from her journal, unaware that it is addressed to God:

> I have no need to write to you or talk to you, you know everything before I can speak, but when one loves, one feels the need to use the same old ways one has always used. I know I am only beginning to love, but already I want to abandon everything, everybody but you. . . .

We are meant to pick up and note the consistent attitudes—the same trust, the same generosity of spirit, the same abandonment. This is true even in the smaller details of the book. Bendrix says of Sarah: "All I noticed about her that first time was her beauty and her happiness and her way of touching people with her hands as though she loved them." And then later we have her cure of Parkis' little boy, ". . . he told the doctor it was Mrs. Miles who came and took away the pain—touching him on the right side of the stomach," and Smythe's facial disfigurement which she cured with a kiss.

We might say that the whole of her "affair" with Bendrix was in essence the same as her subsequent "affair" with God. But having said this one must be immediately aware of its near meaninglessness. God cannot be apprehended as a person, and to convey the transition by shuffling names and saying "one feels the need to use the same old ways one has always used" is hopelessly inadequate.

Bendrix, speaking in the accents of Greene, remarks in a general way:

> The sense of unhappiness is so much easier to convey than that of happiness. In misery we seem aware of our own existence, even though it may be in a form of monstrous egotism: this pain of mine is individual, this nerve that winces belongs to me and no other. But happiness annihilates us: we lose our identity.

This is an interesting passage because it shows Greene stating what looks like a difficulty of communication, but is in fact a philosophical conviction. It is with God, in the aspect of the suffering Christ, that Sarah seeks to identify herself. But to say this is not to say that we can only apprehend the pain of God. When Smythe says bitterly to Sarah of his disfigurement, "Why should I love a God who gives a child this?" she comments: "I shut my eyes and put my mouth against the mark. I felt sick for a moment because I fear deformity, and he sat quiet and let me kiss him and I thought I am kissing pain and pain belongs to you *as happiness never does* (my italics). I love you in your pain. I could almost taste metal and salt in the skin and I thought how good You are. You might have killed us with happiness, but You let us be with You in pain." The trouble with this is that we are in danger of projecting our own pain and calling it the pain of Christ, of building Him in the image of our own unhappiness. Instead of moving outwards towards God, we are assuming Him into our own world, so that he becomes simply another factor in our torments of abandonment, jealousy and loyalty. For Bendrix, Sarah's action is hysteria and her belief is of a kind which would not enable her to contest that description. The upshot of this presentation of Sarah—a presentation emphatic in its stress on disposition rather than act, on the moment rather than duration, on faith rather than morals—is to tend to make Sarah, in her relations with Bendrix, "selfless" to the point of inhumanity, and, in her relations with God, self-projected to the point of delusion.

The fact that the reader feels the portrait of Sarah is more flatteringly lit than this is due largely to the way in which he is persuaded to concur in a particular view of reason and a particular view of faith. "Reason" is most obviously present in the character of Smythe, the rationalist preacher. Critics have remarked on the injustice of Greene's presentation and how he has deliberately given Smythe a crudity of outlook which suggests he is afraid to present the anti-Christian position with proper seriousness and cogency. This protest is only partially valid. Greene is hostile to religious argument, and the attack he mounts, in the person of Smythe, is not so much on the inadequacies of rationalist argument as on the irrelevance of reason to faith. And Smythe's self-defeating rationalism hammers the point home. Too fiercely, however, because the crudity of Smythe's views, however explicable in "life," suggests in fiction that Greene is unwilling to expose Sarah to a mind more subtly sceptical. The ultimate result might well be the same, but the *effect of the process* on the reader would be very different. Greene would reveal that Sarah's faith had been more rigorously tested, and, when it triumphed, its presence would carry a greater reality. In life it is only the triumph that matters, in art it is more the manner of the triumph, even in matters of faith. Here, mirrored in a detail, is the central difficulty of the novel. In Henry, Greene might have taken an opportunity to vary the quality of the sceptic's outlook, but his accents are exactly those of Smythe:

> "Materialism isn't only an attitude for the poor. . . . Some of the best brains have been materialist, Pascal, Newman. So subtle in some directions; so crudely superstitious in others. One day we may know why: it may be a glandular deficiency."

And, lest the point should not have been taken, we have it made again, this time with conscious irony. Sarah wonders:

> "Have I some glandular deficiency that I am so uninterested in the really important unsuperstitious things and causes—like the Charity Commission and the index of living and better calories for the working class?"

But the devaluation of reason is all-pervasive and extends beyond the non-believers. The priest tells Henry and Bendrix about Sarah's intention of becoming a Catholic:

> "Is that enough to make her one?"
> Father Crompton produced a formula. He laid it down like a bank note. "We recognize the baptism of desire."

This is not merely a description of Bendrix's reaction, there is the same quiver of hostility here to debate and explanation as there is in the presentation of the rationalist preacher's polemic.

The clue to this attitude lies in Greene's own experience. "And so faith came to one," he writes in the autobiographical *The Lawless Roads*, "shapelessly without dogma, a presence above a croquet lawn. . . ." Inexplicable, fortuitous, unavoidable, incalculable, this is Greene's presentation of the arrival of belief. The hand of God

is too close for us to understand the kind of gesture it makes.[1] In
The End of the Affair this attitude is conveyed by two repeated
images. The first is of infection. In her last letter to Bendrix,
Sarah writes:

> I believe there's a God—I believe the whole bag of tricks, there's
> nothing I don't believe, they could subdivide the Trinity into a
> dozen parts and I'd believe. They could dig up records. . . . I've
> caught belief like a disease.

And Sarah's mother talking of her child's baptism says:

> "I always had a wish that it would 'take' like vaccination."

Later, Bendrix hears Henry repeat the idea:

> "It's an extraordinary coincidence isn't it? Baptized at two years
> old, and then beginning to go back to what you can't even remem-
> ber. . . . It's like an infection."

The emphasis of this reiterated image is on the passivity of the
individual, the incapacity to resist or encourage this inexplicable
event. Related to this is another image, that of drowning, which
underlines the same attitude. Sarah compares herself to a lost ship,
with the water rising, and the air thick with mist. Bendrix, shaken
in his scepticism by her miraculous intervention in the lives of
others, says: "I felt like a swimmer who has overpassed his strength
and knows the tide is stronger than himself, but if I drowned, I was
going to hold Henry up to the last moment." Spiritual determinism
could hardly go further. Sarah is pursued by the love of Christ as
surely as Tess by the implacable President of the Immortals.
Greene's outlook in *The End of the Affair* finds an admirable gloss
in Mauriac's *La Pharisienne*:

> People do not change. At my age one can have no illusions on
> that point: but they do quite often turn back to what they once
> were and show again those very characteristics which they have
> striven tirelessly through a whole life-time to suppress. This does
> not mean that they necessarily end by succumbing to what is worst
> in themselves. God is very often the good temptation to which
> many human beings in the long run yield.

---

[1] Mauriac is quite explicit about this difficulty: "Whenever a novelist has tried
to re-create the way of grace, with all its struggles and its ultimate victory, he
has left an impression of arbitrariness and mis-representation . . . God is
inimitable and he escapes the novelist's grasp" (*Dieu et Mammon*).

By isolating "reason" and "faith" in this way I have of course given them a prominence which they do not have in the novel. But they are crucial in helping to shape the reader's response to Sarah —and to her Bargain with God.

It is in this central act that the details of her presentation come sharply into focus, so that we are moved into accepting something which, viewed through a less extraordinary lens than that which Greene has employed, would have been quite incomprehensible. The kind of scepticism which has to be overcome is suggested by Smythe's remark, ". . . leave God out of this. It's just a question of your lover and your husband. Don't confuse the thing with phantoms." But given Sarah as she has been presented, we realize that neither Smythe's reasons, nor anyone else's, would move her. If she makes the Bargain, there is also a sense in which the Bargain is made for her.

To begin with it is an affair which belongs purely to "the Moment," and she enters into it with the same complex abandonment as she has entered into her "Moments" with Bendrix. Demanding of God "Make me believe," she has to meet her spiritual liabilities in full, because any kind of hesitation, any kind of reasoned doubt, is alien to her. Her decision is insulated against every reason. There are psychological reasons for breaking her bargain, but if she labels her action "hysterical," her experience tells her she is wrong. Such an "explanation" is only there to protect her from the burden of mystery. On the other hand, there are moral reasons, such as loyalty to Henry, which she might draw on to enable her to maintain her bargain. But a moral appraisal, like a psychological solution, is irrelevant to her. If she didn't feel "guilt" before with Bendrix, she certainly doesn't feel "innocent" without him. Any moral aura which surrounds the bargain is an illusion. It is the promise itself, not the nature of the promise, which is the imperative. It is obvious that with Sarah's bargain we are in the suburbs of Illuminism, where "reason" is taken as synonymous with pride. Whatever prompted and sustained Sarah's pact with God, one thing is abundantly clear: that is that, on its own definition, it can never be shown—only stated.

At this point description of the religious background of the novel begins to shade into literary judgment about its value. Religious orthodoxy, after all, is not synonymous with artistic merit. And in this particular case there seems an intimate connection between its religious emphases and what we must regard as its literary failings. It is important to make clear exactly what kind of point is being made here. There is no *a priori* reason why successful novels should not be written about the life of grace, about saints and sinners. But their success will depend on their power of communicating their drama in human terms; in art there is no other perspective. This assertion is not humanist, but human.

An illustration may clarify the point. In Dostoevsky's *Crime and Punishment* the murderer Raskolnikov excitedly urges a girl who loves him to read him the Bible:

> "Why? You are not a believer, are you? . . ." she whispered softly, gasping a little.
>
> "Read! I want you to!" he insisted. "You used to read to Lizaveta!"
>
> Sonya opened the book and found the place. Her hands shook, her voice failed. Twice she tried to begin, but could not utter the first word.
>
> "Now a certain man was sick, named Lazarus of Bethany . . ." she pronounced at last, with an effort, but after two or three words her voice broke like an over-strained violin string. Her breath caught and her heart laboured.
>
> Raskolnikov had understood why Sonya could not make herself read to him, and the more he understood, the more roughly and irritably he insisted. He knew very well how difficult it was for her to expose and betray all that was *her own*. He understood that those feelings in fact constituted her real long-standing *secret,* cherished perhaps since her girlhood, in the midst of her family, with an unhappy father, a stepmother crazed by grief, and hungry children, in an atmosphere of hideous shrieks and reproaches. At the same time he now knew and knew for certain that although she was troubled and feared something terrible if she were to read now, yet she had a tormenting desire to read, and read for *him* to hear, and read *now,* "whatever might happen afterwards" . . . .

It is difficult to convey the atmosphere of a novel briefly, but even in this extract we feel in the presence of a powerful complex of emotions which are given their particular tension by religious faith. And we are made to feel this through and with Raskolnikov. However mysterious and inexplicable Sonya's faith, it finds expression in human terms. In Greene's own work this has been true. In

The Power and the Glory we are shown, in the working out of a
human conflict, something of what goes into the making of a saint.
But in *The End of the Affair* Greene would seem to have taken
the fundamental mysteriousness of sanctity not simply as the theme,
but as directing its manner of expression also.

To see the implications of this artistic dilemma, it is worth quoting the conclusion of the *Times Literary Supplement* review of the
novel:

> The common-sense point of view is surely that whatever the in-
> ward marks of sanctity, the overruling outward one is that in some
> way the candidate's life should be more than ordinarily edifying. Is
> a married woman who gives up her lover for the love of God a
> saint? As Ibsen's Nora says in almost the opposite context: "Thou-
> sands of women have done so."

The bluff, sardonic note of this is useful because it reveals, in an
obvious way, the critic held fast in the same sort of trap as the
novelist. There is confusion, basically, between "art" and "life."
If we think of *The End of the Affair* as an autobiographical work,
the critic's objections weaken. The life of Mary Magdalen was
not to the outward eye "more than ordinarily edifying," and,
when this criticism was in fact made, it met with a stinging rebuke.
There is no real difficulty in believing that a married woman who
gives up her lover for the love of God could be practising heroic
virtue; martyrdom is not limited by its visibility. If, however, *The
End of the Affair* is considered not as a spiritual autobiography,
but as a novel, then the objections appear rather differently, though
the difference has certainly nothing to do with "the common sense
point of view." In life, we are continually warned against rashness
of judgment, because all the evidence can never be available to us.
In art, *all* that has been created of the fictional world is available
to us. Fictional characters must speak to the reader in the same
way as the psalmist speaks to God: "Thou searchest out my path
and my lying down, and art acquainted with all my ways. For there
is not a word in my tongue, but lo, O Lord, thou knowest it altogether." The reader's judgment can, then, be authoritative in
fiction, in a way in which it never can be in life. In life we have
to accept the adequacy of statement as the clue to the reality of
experience, in art we can demand demonstration. Consequently,

from the *literary* point of view we must agree that "inward marks of sanctity" must be revealed outwardly. Otherwise, the writer is sawing through the plank which supports him.

Earlier in this essay I suggested that Sarah leaves the reader with an impression of her "goodness." Literary examination suggests the difficulty of supporting this. The reason for this contradiction should now be becoming plain. In responding to Sarah's "goodness" we are unwittingly going "outside" the fictional character and substituting in her place an "historical" one. The tone of the book is such that we deceive ourselves into reading Sarah's journal as though it was St. Augustine's *Confessions*. We mistake statement for creation. This reaches its extreme point in the question of the miracles. In life, miracles are claimed to testify to a reality other than themselves, in fiction they can only testify to the reality which has made them occur. One part of the fictional world is being made to allege the inexpressible reality of another. And to try to do this is to confuse the whole nature of fiction.

Although this kind of criticism is strictly literary, and is not shaped by philosophical or theological assumptions, it has nevertheless religious implications. If Greene in *The End of the Affair* has become involved in a situation which exceeds the novelist's province, this is not because of his ambitious theme, but because of the particular way he has laid his religious emphases. An incarnational, sacramental view of Christianity leads to the disclosure of the divine *within* the essential imperfections of the human, but in Greene's view the divine offers a stark alternative to the total corruption of the human. Only grace can bridge the gap—and the action of grace as Greene seems to present it is fortuitous, inexplicable and ultimately unknowable. Literary criticism can have nothing to say on the validity of these views, except in so far as they touch on literature. Greene's view has been present in all his religious novels, giving them their taut, vivid and dramatic outline. If these views disturb us in *The End of the Affair* in a way they do not in the earlier novels, this is because he has taken down the melodramatic scaffolding and directly revealed the beliefs themselves. Seen in this way they seem inimical to the public ordering and the public demonstration which successful fiction requires. In the character of Sarah Greene has created someone whose goodness can be understood only in extra-fictional terms. Within the novel we can point only to moral categories, and these are set aside as irrelevant. Sarah is the "fallen woman" for whom "guilt" and "innocence" are meaningless terms.

In deadening the moral nerve of the novel Greene has made its whole movement, however vivid and compelling in detail, finally unknowable. Unknowable in the way that human beings are, and fictional characters are not. A report on *The End of the Affair* would conclude not that the art was too remote from life, but rather that there was a failure to distinguish between them.

Mr. Greene's Eggs and Crosses

by Frank Kermode

Oh, is God prodigall? hath he spent his store
Of plagues on us, and only now, when more
Would ease us much, doth he grudge misery,
And will not let's enjoy our curse, to dy?

Mr. Graham Greene's new novel [1] is so far below one's expectation that the questions arise, was the expectation reasonable, and has there been any previous indication that a failure of this kind was a possibility? So I have been reading the novels since *The Power and the Glory* (1940) and taking some note of what Mr. Greene's by now numerous commentators have said about them. Here one jostles uncomfortably with Waterbury, the critic in *The End of the Affair*, who loses his girl to Bendrix the novelist, which is an allegory and explains what critics (men of limited potency) may expect if they are unpleasant to their betters. Hence their refined envy; it is very noticeable that the best criticism of Mr. Greene is hostile. He himself seems to find it all distasteful, whether it is the adulatory sort that discovers "buried significance . . . of which I was unaware" or the nasty sort that finds "faults I was tired of facing." But critics write for people, not for novelists; a poet commenting on another's work is far more likely to say a line won't do than that it suggests a corruption of consciousness which ought to be purged; the novelist does not need to be told that his technical shortcomings have large moral implications. If Mr. Greene, as I think, was always, on the evidence of his earlier work, likely to write a big serious novel that

[1] *A Burnt-out Case.*

would die at birth, he knew better than anybody that it was so; this, however, does not excuse Waterbury from doing his bit.

A Burnt-out Case seems to be this novel. Querry, a famous Catholic architect, takes flight from his old life and stops only when he can go no farther, having reached the heart of darkness, a *leproserie* deep in the Congo. His spiritual condition, as he and the devoted but rationalist doctor Colin see it, is parallel to the physical state of a leper in whom the disease, treated too late, has had to run its course; though technically cured he is mutilated, a burnt-out case. Querry is given such a patient as his servant; and when this man runs off into the bush, in search of some lost paradise, Querry follows him and saves his life, watching with him all night. This act, and some modest building operations undertaken for the priests who run the settlement, seem to be working for the restoration of Querry's humanity. But the diagnosis of Querry and Colin is not accepted by some other characters, notably Fr. Thomas, an unstable priest, Rycker, a detestably pious margarine manufacturer, once a seminarist, and Parkinson, a corrupt English journalist. In pressing home his complaint against Rycker, whose high-minded gossip has proved a serious nuisance, Querry is involved with Rycker's unhappy young wife; instead of seducing her he spends the night telling her the story of his life, got up rather archly as a sort of fairy tale. Hating her husband, she announces that Querry is the father of the child she is carrying, and the consequence of this affair, totally anomalous because Querry has been a selfish and successful lover of women, is that Rycker shoots his rival. Querry dies amused at the irony of this; his power over women was always an index of his worldly success, and when he renounced success he renounced women too; but he dies their victim.

This fable is constructed with economy and skill. It is a characteristic Greene plot (though less complex than some), for it turns upon a point of comedy, or farce—the husband-wife-lover situation which occurs in a considerable variety of manifestations in the later Greene, and with special ingenuity in *The End of the Affair* and *The Complaisant Lover*. (This time the lover is pitying, impotent, and bores the wife all night.) The timing of the story is very exact; the burnt-out leper is not too obtrusive, the talk with the girl is dramatically well-placed, and the catastrophe is arranged like an expert final act: an innocent champagne party with the priests celebrating the erection of a roof-tree on Querry's building, the approaching storm, the arrival of the Ryckers, which ends the story by destroying not only Querry's life but his growing reputation for sanctity. The clinical details of leprosy are tactfully disposed though shocking in the right degree ("the sweet smell of sloughed skin") and the descriptions of tropical river and bush have the moody accuracy one has learned to expect. The idiom is often satisfyingly Greeneian—there is an ample provision of those new proverbs of hell: "it was God's taste to be worshipped and their taste to worship, but only at stated hours like a suburban embrace on a Saturday night"; "suffering is something which will always be provided when required"; and there are some of those sad recondite conceits: "The pouches under his eyes were like purses that contained the smuggled memories of a disappointing life." Everywhere there is evidence of competent arrangements. It is arranged, for instance, that we should not like the priests, yet be forced to meditate on their view of the meaning of the events described. If the texture of these events is thinner than in, say, *The Heart of the Matter,* that merely makes clearer the theme of the book; the problem is not to find a way of saying what this is, but rather to account for the discrepancy between it and the story, the failure to give it a body.

The theme, to name it accurately but perhaps misleadingly, is Heroic Virtue. This term is used during a conversation between Colin and the dreadful, stubborn Fr. Thomas in the lull before the stormy climax of the book. Fr. Thomas is saying what a good thing it was for them that Querry had dropped in and put up this new building. Colin observes that it was an even better thing for Querry himself, who is now almost cured. Fr. Thomas at once reduces Querry's history to a familiar theological term: "the better the man the worse the aridity." He has been determined, ever since he found out who Querry was, to understand him in this language and no other. The doctor protests that they have no application to Querry's case; but the priest answers that whereas the doctor is trained to spot the early symptoms of leprosy, the priest is expert in detecting incipient Heroic Virtue. This is one of the best scenes in the book, full of ironies, little time-bombs planted with short fuses among the illusory satisfactions of the evening; and not the least striking of them is the implicit analogy between leprosy and Heroic Virtue. Fr. Thomas does not use the expression loosely; he has in mind the teaching of the Church on this subject, which, if I understand it, is pretty definite. Between the "political" or "social" virtues and the "divine" or "exemplary" virtues—between the human and the divine—there are intermediate virtues of two degrees of perfection, the first of which are called purifying (*purgatoriae*) and the second "the virtues of the purified soul" (*virtutes iam purgati animi*). Fr. Thomas presumably supposes Querry's bad time to have corresponded to the first of these states, and his present conduct to the second. The condition of Heroic Virtue is distinguished from that of sanctity, though officially described as "rare in this life." Fr. Thomas, in short, is putting Querry pretty high, and in terms of a doctrine which means nothing to Colin or to Querry himself. The situation is characteristic of the author, who is constantly pointing out that human behaviour acquires an entirely different and often disturbing valuation when you consider it in the light of religious doctrine; and the question here is whether you ought to do so, especially when that doctrine is applied mechanically by vulgar and imperceptive people, including priests.

For this religious interpretation of Querry's life is applied by others, and indeed it is the cause of the crisis of the plot. The practice was started by Rycker with his vulgar lust for holiness; then Fr. Thomas odiously takes it up, with his theory of aridity: "Perhaps even now you are walking in the footsteps of St. John of the Cross, the *noche oscura*." He can't get it into their heads that he is merely burnt out. The journalist Parkinson, vulgarized beyond any hope that he might recognize distinctions between truth and falsehood, wants to make of Querry a Sunday-paper Schweitzer, even a saint if that will please Them (his readers). "I wouldn't be surprised if there were pilgrims at your shrine in twenty years, and that's how history's written. *Exegi monumentum.* Quote. Virgil." But divine intervention in human affairs is, as we could have learnt from Mr. Greene, apparently capricious, often tasteless, and quite capable of working through Rycker or Parkinson. Even Colin has his doubts about Querry: "You're too troubled by your lack of faith. . . . You keep on fingering it like a sore." And Querry himself remembers, "in moments of superstition," that there are religious explanations for his condition; for instance, he thinks that in choosing art he deliberately forfeited grace, a point Fr. Thomas would confute simply by indicating his good works.

On the whole, however, Querry offers naturalist explanations only, and these, of course, conflict with the others. This is the choice the book offers. Either Querry is right, or God is a plot-maker, working through his inferior priests, through the theological pervert Rycker, through innocence and pity (great enemies of human happiness in Greene); ready to use any degree of absurdity— an incompetent private detective, a preposterous Palais Royal bedroom scene, to get His way. And this is only the crisis; before it God has, on this view, been fostering Querry's self-disgust, making him more and more successful, more and more powerful with women, so as to get him ready for the last strategem.

This is perfectly all right; what goes wrong is the presentation of Querry's alternative explanation. He has recovered from the sickness of faith, and may be getting over the sickness of success. But his way of life has hardened all within and petrified the feeling. He has a dream (Mr. John Atkins in his book reminds us of the extraordinary number of explanatory dreams Mr. Greene's characters have) in which he makes this point: "I can't feel at all, I'm a leper." The one thing he is sure of is that his state has nothing to do with vitality, nobility, or spiritual depth, yet there is this conspiracy to enforce the theory that it has. His identity is discovered in the first place through a cover-drawing in *Time* magazine, which romanticized his features and gave him a soulful, mysterious quality; this is an experience Mr. Greene has had himself. And this is the really important point. Querry, the famous Catholic architect, is a famous Catholic writer thinly disguised; and if it was ever true—as Mr. Greene's hostile critics insist—that the earlier novels are sometimes flawed by the author's inability to stand clear of his hero or victim, it is certainly true of this book.

In one of his long conversations with Colin, Querry explains that he never built except for his own pleasure, and perhaps never loved a woman except for the same reason. "A writer doesn't write for his readers, does he? . . . The subject of a novel is not the plot." He makes buildings (books) in which people can be comfortable, but he is not interested in their use, and hardly minds when they are clogged with cheap ornaments (the irrelevant personal rubbish a reader might bring to a book to make it seem lived-in). The real object of writing (building) is selfish: "Self-expression is a hard and selfish thing. It eats everything, even the self. At the end you find you haven't even got a self to express. I have no interest in anything. . . . I don't want to sleep with a woman or design a building." The difficulty is that Querry's self-explanation is a mere diagram; he has chosen a self-consuming artist's life, perfection of the work. Even when he is drawn into the service of suffering he protests that "Human beings are not my country." For the doctrine of the priests he substitutes not nature but a myth of decadence; there is even a secular version of Fr. Thomas's smug theory of aridity in his talk of the artist's regress. One is driven towards the position taken up by Miss Elizabeth Sewell in a remarkable essay on Mr. Greene published a few years ago in the *Dublin Review*: he is a novelist of the Decadence, writing not as a Catholic but as a neo-Romantic. His heroes, all *maudits,* know nothing of the happiness and hope that are, after all, part of religion; his world is one in which only Faust can be saved, and the victimized postures of his heroes are ulti-mately Faustian. I should want to modify Miss Sewell's account of the basic myth, but there seems no doubt that Querry, more than any other of the heroes, is a poseur, and ought not to be if the conflict between religious and secular interpretations of his life is to have a valid basis.

This issue becomes very acute in the fairy-tale version of his life which Querry tells Mme Rycker to put her to sleep. Reviewers have called this embarrassing; yet it is the marrow of the book. It ex-poses the falsity of Querry's position, not because the stupid priests are necessarily right, but because their view of the matter can be fully and ironically presented but this decadent mythology cannot. He speaks of a man who has not been able to detect the hand of God in human life; who sees virtue rewarded by the death of a child (the crucial test of God in *The Heart of the Matter*) and viciousness punished only invisibly. Instead of being a great artist he became a sort of Fabergé, making ingenious jewels and enjoying many women. God refused to allow him to suffer. But although people thought he must be very good to have such rewards from God—as others who got their legs cut off in accidents must be very bad—he found that, unable to suffer, he was unable to love. His jewels were fashionable, and people said he was not only a master-technician but dealt with serious subject-matter, because he made eggs with gold crosses on top, "set with precious stones in honour of the King." About this time a mistress committed suicide, without his being much disturbed. Then, as popular favour waned, the connoisseurs took him up. "They began to write books about his art; especially those who claimed to know and love the King" calling him, for instance, "the Jeweller of Original Sin." For "jeweller" one reads "architect = Querry = novelist = ?" (Mr. Greene has said before that a novel is always a kind of confession.) At this point the jeweller sees that his work has nothing to do with love, the love of the King for his people; and he wonders, as the whole plot of Mr. Greene's novel does, whether his unbelief and the ugliness of his success are not finally proof of the King's existence. While he has been talking the night away the King has in fact been at work, in the shape of the prying Parkinson, ensuring that this "success" will amount in the end to the same thing as failure, that so much more desirable fate. Only failures can be good, and God is a specialist in failure. Querry is to have his suffering; "with suffering we become part of the Christian myth." He dies not for his own crimes but for those of the Ryckers; as in *The Heart of the Matter* this is a case of *victimage,* like Huysmans refusing morphia for cancer of the throat.

The artist's lust for suffering can be called a leading theme of Mr. Greene's. There is a hint of it in the famous autobiographical piece, "The Revolver in the Corner Cupboard." Since the acceptance of God entails pain, it is a theme to be found in *The End of the Affair.* It is strongly present in this book, a dominant, but not fully embodied theme; and behind it is something less easy to extract, the persistent notion of God as the enemy, whose disastrous invasion of human life is called by theologians love. Let us look, without making too much of it, at the little emblem of the egg-jewel with the cross on top. On the world of natural generations is stuck, incongruous, the heraldic device of God. Mr. Greene's books are like that. We could get along, better perhaps since He is so interested in pain, without God. Scobie's situation would have been tolerable if the egg had no cross; his wife uses the pledge of God's love to torment him, and out of love he comes to death; even death is worse with God, since one cannot take it out of His hands without wounding Him. (To the non-believer like Fowler in *The Quiet American* death is something one may reasonably desire, like sex, though, virgins all, we may be scared of it as well as attracted.) The harshness of Mr. Greene's Christianity is that the unforgivable sins are the most tempting, and that however unreasonable God may be He is also strong, and has somehow convinced us that He is easily hurt. How much easier to be a Stoic! Sometimes it seems that the disaster—that aboriginal calamity—that fell upon us was not the Fall but God (who foresaw without willing it). Ever since His arrival on the scene the good human emotions, and chiefly pity, are dangerous, innocence an evil trap. Querry is only the last of Greene heroes to be caught in it. They belong only to the nursery paradise, not to the wild woods forlorn of the fallen. Scobie has to pray *not* to be a decent fellow, but to do the will of a master who allows children to die after surviving forty days in a ship's boat, so that he may save his soul; but pity frustrates him. The priest in *The Power and the Glory* is obsessed with the need to protect God from himself. Sin is the shadow thrown by the strong light of God; Mr. Greene is of the devil's party and comes near to knowing it. God's priests are rarely up to much; the natural man has little time for the voluntary eunuch. This only strengthens the case against Him; He has made us as we are and expects us, on terrible penalties, to behave otherwise; He would not leave us in the state of the amoeba, yet He denies us adult brains. "Why did he give us genitals if he wanted us to think clearly?" ("Vainly begot, and yet forbidden vanity, Created sick, commanded to be sound.") Once the intellect accepts God (Mr. Greene has emphasized that his reception into the Church was a result of intellectual rather than emotional conviction) a terrible incongruity invades human affairs; confronted with that image human sex becomes fury and mire. The natural man can scarcely act without alienating Him; there is even a feeling that the ugly shapes of the world are caused by this constraint. Yet if He wants heroes, He has to find them among the dying generations; He must work in the fury and the mire. *A Burnt-out Case* may be read as an account of His doing so, confronted with a naturalist account of the same events.

The resultant tension might make a great book; it does not have that effect here, or anywhere else except in *The End of the Affair*.

The Power and the Glory sometimes comes near to a full realization, with its well-placed sermon on pain and fear as "part of
heaven," the paradoxical emphasis on the beauty of sin, especially
sexual sin (as in the passage with the pious old maid and the shameless copulators in prison) and the perversely high valuation put
upon suffering. The priest's surprised admission that his enemy, the
lieutenant, is "a good man," and the determined irrationalism of
his conduct, especially at the crisis, silently stress the obsessive
theme, the use God makes of wantonly unsuitable material for
humanly detestable ends. And, as nearly always in Mr. Greene,
the concept of mortal sin, so incredible on the human view of
decency, is continually eroded by reservations of all sorts. But it
is true that this endless complaint about God seems less to be
shaping the book than tearing it apart, and I think it is on this
score that *The Power and the Glory* has had some damaging criticism, notably from F. N. Lees, who thinks it never becomes "the
study of will and conduct" it seems to aim at being, but sinks into
"self-condemnatory reverie"; instead of an "evaluating vision of
a situation" we get a ventriloquial performance with an interesting
dummy. Mr. Lees argues from evidences of strain in the language
of the book; Mr. Hoggart, with a very nice understanding of its
qualities, comes nevertheless, though from a different direction,
to the same conclusion: "we are in the presence of an unusually
controlled allegory. . . . The characters have a kind of life, but
that life is always breathed into them by Greene's breath. In
Greene's novels we do not "explore experience"; we met Graham
Greene." Though I think both these criticisms are too severe, one
sees what brought them into being; Mr. Greene's war against the
intolerable God his intellect accepts is an extremely personal matter, and its obsessive presence is felt everywhere, colouring, distort-
ing, taking the place of, more generalized "experience," suggesting
that "will and conduct" are only defensive tactics in the struggle
with omnipotence.

It would seem that the way out of this is to objectify the obsession, to embody the God-hatred in the fiction. *The Heart of the
Matter* in a way does this; much of the torment comes from the
position that natural knowledge, knowledge of sex, is real, and
knowledge of God by comparison notional; if you abuse a

woman she will be hurt or angry, but you can insult and debase God without His giving any sign. So a man damns himself out of pity for those who cry out; that, at any rate, is what the rules say, and if there is an escape clause ("the appalling strangeness of the mercy of God") we cannot be sure of its application. Scobie is Greene's greatest expert in proverbs of hell, in "the loyalty we all feel to unhappiness—the sense that that is where we really belong." He is cursed by an awareness of "the weakness of God" and by integrity-destroying pity; sufficiently of God's party to know that failure alone is lovable, but critical of the divine arrangements. ("Couldn't we have committed our first major sin at seven, have ruined ourselves for love or hate at ten, have clutched at redemption on a fifteen-year-old death-bed?") Consequently, "as for God, he could speak to Him only as one speaks to an enemy." In the end he propagates suffering instead of preventing it by total self-sacrifice, because God will not allow one to arrange the happiness of others as one wishes. As to the "eternal sentence" which our intellectual knowledge of God insists to have been Scobie's due, it is pronounced for an act of which the human significance is trivial, the theft of a little bread. But of course there is Fr. Rank to say we do not understand God, that Scobie's conduct may be divinely construed as love of God. Mr. Lees observes with severity that this remark is misplaced, since we know, as God does, what has gone on in Scobie's mind, and "if at his death we don't know that he *won't* go to Heaven, we most certainly don't know that he *will*." This is part of a charge that the novelist gives uncritical assent to Scobie's "shouldering of the world's whole weight," and indeed he is a classic case of *victimage,* with the priest brought in to say that nobody can affirm this "decadent" position to be erroneous. But I do not see that there is total identification of author and character here; the point of the revelation that Mrs. Scobie knew very well what she was doing when she coaxed her erring husband to Mass is that he was wanting in self-knowledge in a matter where you would expect a policeman not to be; he bungles an ordinary appraisal of human suspicion; and to this extent Mr. Greene is saying that Scobie had a *wrong* idea of himself. But the main issue of the book is not fully discussed: it is that Scobie's intolerable position is plotted by God; He demands more love and pity than anybody else and ought not to get them. Even specialists

in Him know far more about His demands than about His bene-
factions; it is His mercy, not His justice, that is unfamiliar, "appallingly strange." A good man should not be treated as Scobie is. But
all this lurks immediately under the surface of the book's argument;
the egg is not allowed to speak out against the Cross.

This speaking out was delayed until *The End of the Affair,* and
this seems almost beyond question Mr. Greene's masterpiece, his
fullest and most completely realized book. Mr. Lees says the opening paragraph is uneasily slack; but in a deliberately tentative way
it disposes of a remarkable amount of information. A novelist, a
good technician launching what purports to be a straightforward
narrative but at the same time foreseeing Conradian complexities,
hesitates deliberately over the arbitrary but necessary starting-
point; and he wants the essential fact of his being a writer, and
the other essential fact of his new, odious, belief in God, to get said
at once. Bendrix is not a Scobie but the hero Mr. Greene has
needed: a natural man who sees this God as a natural man would,
as unscrupulous rival, corrupter of human happiness, spoiler of the
egg; and a novelist who hates Him as a superior technician.
Bendrix's book is plotted by God, a testimony to His structural
powers. And we get for the first and only time the real Satanic
thing, the courage never to submit or yield. All this is germinal in
the first page, which contains sentences crucial to the entire *œuvre:*
"If hate is not too large a term to use in relation to any human
being, I hated Henry." . . . "He surely must have hated his wife
and that other, in whom in those days *we were lucky enough not
to believe.*" Bendrix's fury in the end is that of the trapped: everything from onions to the absurd private detective, the rationalist
lectures, Arbuckle Avenue, flying bombs, miracles that can be explained away, is economically employed by the Plotter. And just as
Bendrix is a potent enough novelist to take away the critic's girl,
God is a good enough one to take away his, even though she doesn't
want to go; He plants in her not only love of Him but His favourite
Augustinian reluctance (". . . but not yet") to increase the pain.
"Dear God, you know I want Your pain, but I don't want it now."

The unwilling sanctification of Sarah is a difficult theme, and
leads the novelist into some expressions that may seem excessive,
though hardly ever in the rapt context; and God's perversity and
skill are remembered even by Sarah, who takes the deforming

strawberry mark as His image, and remembers how unfairly He used Bendrix to His own ends. It is a mark of the difference of this book that the last words are shared between the frigid priest and Bendrix, and Bendrix is very explicit: "I know Your cunning. It's You who take us up to a high place and offer us the whole universe. You're a devil, God, tempting us to leap." He can no longer refuse to believe in the disastrous existence of God; but he can still separate the idea from love. But God may not have finished with him. This is another love-triangle, but even the hate necessarily generated may be converted by Him into an inhuman love. The book ends with Bendrix praying for the peace of the natural man, burnt out. It is the only novel to offer a full statement of the case for the fornicating human victim, for the energy as well as the sadness of hell, and the case against the God who inflicts, as with love, that pain from which the pleasure-loving flesh continually shrinks. Mr. Lees calls Bendrix an evil man, and the book gives him some right to do so; but this reminds one again of the genuine proverb of hell, that hell is energy; and the difference between the vicious energy of Bendrix and the rigidly self-conscious despair of Querry is a fair measure of the difference in quality between the two books. Querry is too clearly a surrogate; the argument about Heroic Virtue is also a substitute, too partial, too technical perhaps, to bear the weight of the real theme: natural happiness, defeated not by success or surfeit, but by God and His love.

The Uncomplacent Dramatist:
Some Aspects of
Graham Greene's Theatre

by *Philip Stratford*

It is interesting to speculate what makes an outstanding novelist turn playwright and especially, as in Graham Greene's case,
when the change in genre coincides with some important develop-
ments in artistic outlook. Although Greene's reputation was made
in the novel, he has always been interested in the dramatic form.
From 1935 to 1941 he reviewed films and plays regularly for *The
Spectator*. In 1937 he was film editor for *Night and Day*. In 1942 he
published a short book on the history of English drama. It was not
until after the war, however, that his critical interest turned creative. While gaining valuable experience in cinema (he has written,
supplied or collaborated on scripts for almost twenty screen plays
to date), he wrote his first play, *The Living Room*, in 1953. This
has been followed by two others, *The Potting Shed* (1957) and *The
Complaisant Lover* (1959), each of which shows increasing mastery
of the new medium.

This growing interest in legitimate theatre corresponds to a
gradual change in the character of Greene's fiction. Little by little
the pre-war violence, melodrama and morality have been sup-
pressed. After *The Living Room* religious themes drop into the
background. Of sex, war, and crime, the other main ingredients of
his novels, only sex remains in the plays where murder has been
replaced by adultery and the outlaw by the illicit lover. The exotic,

subtropical settings of novels and entertainments have given way to the mundane upper-middle-class living room. Characters are no longer drawn from the substrata of society but become respectable business or professional men, university lecturers, journalists, antiquarian book dealers and dentists. All the plays are psychological studies set in a domestic situation, but from *The Living Room* to *The Complaisant Lover* there is a definite movement away from tragedy and towards sophisticated comedy.

To consider this development in the light of Greene's early criticism of drama and films sharpens and dramatizes the change. These reviews reveal an outspoken young writer convinced of the seriousness of art and capable of stigmatizing the insincere and the second-rate with wit and acumen. In one of his early critical pieces Greene quotes Chekhov: "The best artists are realistic and paint life as it is, but because every line is permeated, as with a juice, by awareness of a purpose, you feel, besides life as it is, also life as it ought to be." And throughout his reviews he bases his own judgment on this dual standard of realism and criticism.

This accounts for the severity of Greene's treatment of popular dramatists in the thirties. Either they represented "no more of life than a holiday snapshot," or, if they had some idea of life as it should be, expressed it "only in terms of sexual or financial happiness." As for film writing, Greene called it "the novelist's Irish sweep: money for no thought, for the banal situation and the inhuman romance: money for forgetting how people live." Against the falsity of "popular" commercialism Greene upheld the ideal of "a genuinely vulgar art," an art "as popular and unsubtle as a dance tune" which would "dive below the polite level to something nearer common life." This view supported well what he was trying to do in his own fiction at the time, and explains his choice of the brand of popular melodrama which made him famous. But even in his "entertainments" the critical sense of life as it should be was never absent. "If you excite your audience first," he wrote, "you can put over what you will of horror, suffering, truth."

In *British Dramatists* (1942) he set his critical theories in an historical context. As he traces its development from mystery and morality, Greene praises those qualities in English drama that are deeply rooted in the experience of the common people: a vigorous confrontation with the hard facts of life, a sense of destiny, and the

quick recognition of "the dark side of human nature," and he de-
plores the softening which sets in when the theatre ceases to be
anything "but the recreation of the educated, the aristocratic . . .
and the well-to-do." He uses Shakespeare as prototype of the popular genius. Not only does his work embody the vitality and realism
of common life, but it reaches back to the morality with its sense
of ritual and its simple but powerful abstractions. In Shakespeare,
Greene writes, "the abstraction (Revenge, Jealousy, Ambition, In-
gratitude) still rules the play. And rightly. Here is the watershed
between morality and the play of character: the tension between the
two is perfectly kept. There is dialectical perfection." After Shakespeare and the Jacobeans, character wins "too costly a victory."
The religious sense is lost; sentimentality creeps in to falsify life
as it is, and the happy ending to undermine the sense of life as it
should be; personal idiosyncrasy replaces universal passions; plot
takes precedence over theme, and the realist revival rejuvenates
the stage only in the sense that it provides a middle-class public
with new subject matter. These are the terms that Greene chooses
to discuss the evolution of the drama from morality, "the bones
without the flesh," to contemporary theatre which is so often "flesh
without the bones."

Now, despite the vigour and consistency of this criticism, Greene
considerably modified his attitude after the war. Setting the development of his own work against the historical background of
British Dramatists, one could say that gradually his popular Web-
ster-like fiction—"violent, universal tragedies" heavy with religious
implications and best characterized by *Brighton Rock*—gives way
to a domestic drama which owes something to Henry James and
is more closely designed for a well-to-do, middle-class public, as for
example *The End of the Affair.* And although realism and criticism
are still present, his latest play, *The Complaisant Lover,* resembles
in many respects the "popular" drawing room comedy which he
himself had handled so harshly in the thirties.

One can begin to trace this change in *The Heart of the Matter*
(1948). Although this novel drew on a tropical setting for atmosphere like *The Power and the Glory* (1940), it was much more
closely fashioned, with fewer characters and less action; the pattern
of pursuit remained but was turned from exterior to interior; the
central problem no longer had social or political overtones but

remained firmly psychological. In this novel Greene treated the theme of pity as he had in his wartime thriller, *The Ministry of Fear,* but he eschewed many of his familiar melodramatic devices, and although the war figures in both novels, in *The Heart of the Matter* it is subdued and distant.

In all these respects there is further development in the same direction with the next novel, *The End of the Affair* (1951). There is a narrowing compass of action and a tightening of situation— technically this is Greene's most complex novel, but also the most unified, written entirely from the first person viewpoint. There is less dependence on setting—not Africa but London, and not the seedy squalor of earlier London novels but suburban propriety. And as in the following dramas there is an ever more penetrating analysis of conduct in a domestic situation.

From the evidence of these novels alone one could predict that the dramatic form stood in the direct line of his development. The limiting of action, the deepening of insight into character, the domestication of setting and atmosphere, the increase in quantity and flexibility of dialogue all point to the challenge of the three unities, an action single and complete and of a certain magnitude, and the author alive only in his characters.

Certain factors are circumstantial to this change in emphasis. As a young writer eager to make his mark Greene had no fear of over- stating his critical theories, and of course, they were all grist to the mill as far as his own fiction was concerned. But eight novels afterwards he had sufficiently proved himself, and maturity and success had somewhat blunted the edge of his enthusiasm for popu- lar art. The war, too, which Greene saw as an almost apocalyptic outbreak of universal violence, slaked his craving for fictional ex- citement. And finally, after 1945, what interest he retained in popu- lar melodrama was diverted into a new medium, the cinema.

But even here Greene's growing impatience with film work is symptomatic of his shift in interest towards the drama. He has spoken of script-writing slightingly as simply a means of livelihood. "It's a pretty distressing business," he writes, "for when all is said and done, a writer's part in making a film is relatively small." He resents losing control over his story, dislikes the impersonality of the studio, has frequently announced that he would write no more scenarios, and after work on a film speaks of returning with relief to the novel, "that one-man business where I bear full responsibility for failure."

In contrast he has written glowingly of his "very happy" introduction to the theatre:

> I had not anticipated the warmth, the amusement and the comradeship, the delight of working with players interested not only in their own parts but with the play as a whole (a film actor is hardly aware of what happens when he is not on the set), nearly a dozen lively informed intelligences criticizing the suggesting . . . . Above all I had not realized that the act of creation, as with the novel, would continue so long after the first draft of the play was completed, that it would extend through rehearsals and through the preview week. It is for the act of creation that one lives . . . .

There is one other reason for Greene's new fascination with drama. "The interest in the technicalities of his art can alone prevent the mind dulling, the imagination losing power," he wrote as early as 1933. "Nothing else can enable an author to approach each new book with sustained intellectual excitement." And reviewing Leon Edel's edition of *The Plays of Henry James,* although he makes clear that James's primary motives for trying the new form were fame and money (not to be overlooked as motives for Greene himself), he sees James "challenged as any artist by a new method of expression. The pride and interest of attempting the new possessed him." More modestly and more whimsically he excuses his own experiments in drama with the phrase "One must try every drink once," but clearly it is the technical challenge which in his maturity has tempted him to experiment in the most objective and exigent of literary forms.

Within Greene's plays themselves one can observe a development of a different sort. The first of these, *The Living Room,* carries on the line of the Catholic novels. It deals with a love affair tragically complicated by religion as in *The Heart of the Matter* or *The End of the Affair.* Its bitter lover, unappealing wife, long-suffering young mistress, and ineffectual priest are stock Greene characters whose roles have been newly apportioned and whose situation has been transposed to the stage. His next play, *The Potting Shed,* investigates a familiar theme, the problem of identity. Greene calls it "a drama" and although the play resembles the entertainment more than the Catholic novel, it is a psychological thriller that moves backward into memory rather than the usual wide-ranging story of pursuit and evasion. The third play, *The Complaisant Lover,* swings most completely out of the orbit of standard Greene fiction. For the first time religion is entirely absent; for the first time Greene gives a sympathetic, full-scale portrait, not only of mistress and lover, but also of the deceived husband; for the first time his vision is comic. Its very title reminiscent of Restoration comedy, *The Complaisant Lover* is much closer to Webster's *A Cure for a Cuckold* than to his more typical melodrama *The White Devil.*

Tragedy, drama, comedy,—"One must try every drink once." But more significantly, this development within the genre complements the chastening of style, the domestication of subject matter and the growing objectivity in treatment that we have already noted as Greene turns from the narrative form to the dramatic. The introduction of comedy in Greene's work, however, is not peculiar to the plays, and before examining *The Complaisant Lover* in detail as the latest and most revealing example of his new dramatic skills and outlook, one should briefly trace his increasingly bold use in recent fiction of a latent comic gift.

Long accomplished in sketching minor characters with a blend of grotesque humour and pathos—Minty in *England Made Me,* Mr. Tench in *The Power and the Glory,* Harris in *The Heart of the Matter,* to cite only a few—Greene first gave this type a major role in *The End of the Affair.* The divorce court detective, Parkis, is gently ridiculed in this novel but survives as a full-bodied comic character quite unlike any earlier detective or police officer. Having once travestied one of his serious archetypal figures, he was to do so again by making the detective a teenage girl in *The Potting Shed* and by creating the comic secret service agent Hawthorne in *Our Man in Havana.* He also began to make light of other stock characters in the fifties. The innocent involved in violence and espionage—Coral Musker in *Stamboul Train,* Anne Crowder in *A Gun for Sale,* Arthur Rowe, Scobie, all treated seriously in the early thrillers—becomes Wormold the sad clown hero of *Our Man in Havana.* The ominous figure of the financier—Sir Marcus in *A Gun for Sale,* Yusef in *The Heart of the Matter*—becomes the worldly-wise but no longer reprehensible "Gom" in *Loser Takes All* where the bitter lover and his naive young mistress are also treated for the first time with light satire, their lovers' quarrel ending humourously and happily.

Perhaps the best example of the new comic twist to Greene's point of view is provided in his latest novel, *A Burnt-Out Case*. This is his most important book since *The End of the Affair*, but it is not, as some critics have said, a return to the type of his earlier "Catholic" fiction. In this novel Greene pointedly ridicules many of the stock religious responses to his work; despite the Congo setting and the themes of adultery and sainthood, it is Querry, hero of the novel, who directs the reader's interpretation and consistently plays down the melodramatic possibilities of the story; and although at the end of the book he is shot in dramatically heightened circumstances, he dies laughing at himself in a situation which one of the characters likens to a Palais Royal farce.

One further example, this time drawn from Greene's drama, will emphasize the change towards a comic vision of life. Suicide, a recurrent theme, is treated tragically in *The Living Room* and in four earlier novels. It is present, but abortive, in the last two plays. In *The Potting Shed* the hero's salvation lies in the release of his repressed memory of a boyhood suicide attempt. In *The Complaisant Lover* the deceived husband considers suicide but, "the district is wrong for tragedy," he decides. "It's unfair, isn't it, that we're only dressed for a comedy."

One could interpret this last remark as a sly author's aside directed to the earnest student of his work. Indeed, the critic who is trying to establish the pattern of continuity in the shifting spectrum of Greene's fiction may well find it "unfair" that Greene himself has said so little to illuminate the change. What is the exact nature of that sidelong step, one would like to ask, which leads an author from considering the world absurd to thinking it funny. Remembering that Greene has warned against underestimating the consistency of his work, does he still think of his plays, and particularly his comedy, as controlled by that "ruling passion which gives to a shelf of novels the unity of a system?" What artistic conversion or personal experience has led him from taking himself seriously to writing a near-parody of his serious work? But, as Greene once wrote of Shakespeare, "biographical rumours lead one nowhere, the important thing is the plays," and following this lead one can turn to *The Complaisant Lover* itself for a key to understanding the uncomplacent dramatist.

Victor Rhodes, *le mari cocu* of the play, is a practical joker and a bore. Dribbling glass, musical cushion, the plastic rat, the tiresome anecdote and the tired joke are the paraphernalia which serve to make him a suitably foppish victim for abuse. But in the first scene it is Clive Root, the lover, who has unwillingly come to dinner, who is the victim of his host's pleasantries. He is caught by the fake burning cigar and narrowly saved by his hostess and mistress, Mary Rhodes, from the musical box under the armchair cushion which plays "Auld Lang Syne." Although Victor in the course of the evening is "hoist with his own petard" and forced to drink from the dribbling glass he intended for Root, he is still in charge of the joke when, alone at the end of the scene, he hunts out the musical box, slips it under the cushion again and "sits down for a moment to try it out, a blissful look upon his face."

The irony of this curtain is apparent to the audience as they watch a hoax of another kind develop, this time with Victor as victim. Mary and her lover plan to deceive the dentist-husband and spend four days together in Holland, and the second scene opens on the morning of the fourth day in their hotel bedroom in Amsterdam.

As their affair develops Greene refuses every temptation to treat it melodramatically. The accessories to the deception—Mary's invented friend and travelling companion with the nursery rhyme name of Jane Crane, the bewildered hotel valet who becomes corespondent in the adultery without knowing which is lover, which husband—these farcical elements like the false burning cigar and the fake bleeding finger keep the affair from degenerating into tragedy. Victor himself unwittingly turns the lovers' deception into a joke when he barges unexpected and unsuspecting into their hotel bedroom with a business acquaintance, Dr. van Droog, who can speak no English. "He's not satisfied with moving into our room and our bed," says Clive bitterly, "he has to make it a cheap farce with his Dutch manufacturer of dental instruments. We aren't allowed a tragedy nowadays without a banana-skin to slip on and make it funny."

The second act, back in the Rhodes' London home, rings further changes on the practical joke. Victor discovers the adultery from a

letter which Clive, in anger, had dictated to the hotel valet in
Amsterdam. The misspellings and incongruities of the letter itself
belie the seriousness of its message. After the scene of discovery
Victor, left alone, "without thinking what he is doing collapses
on the musical chair and puts his face in his hands. The chair starts
playing 'Auld Lang Syne,' but Victor doesn't hear. He is crying
behind his hands."

This is the high point of pathos in the play and hereafter the
pendulum swings back towards comedy. In the next scene Victor,
seeking refuge from the cocktail party that is in progress, is discovered by his twelve-year-old son, Robin, who apprehends something of his father's distress and sympathizes with him.

> *Robin*. It's not a very good party, is it, as parties go?
> *Victor*. No?
> *Robin*. There's sort of a mood around.
> *Victor*. What kind of mood?
> *Robin*. Like the last act in *Macbeth*. "Tomorrow and tomorrow and
> tomorrow."
> *Victor*. Couldn't you be a bit more precise?
> *Robin*. Everybody seems to be expecting something—something like
> the wood coming to Dunsinane.

But Victor tells his confidant: "This isn't *Macbeth*," and later
he remembers the conversation when his thoughts turn to suicide.
We learn that he has gone to the garage:

> "I only wanted to be alone, so I sat in the car," he explains to Mary
> afterwards. "Then I remembered something I had read in the
> papers. I turned the engine on. I shut the garage doors. But the
> word 'silly' came to my mind . . . and the headline in the news-
> paper. 'Love Tragedy in West Drayton.' This isn't West Drayton,
> but the district is wrong for tragedy too . . . . A suicide looks better
> in a toga, and carbon monoxide poisoning is not exactly a Roman
> death. I thought of Macbeth." "Why Macbeth?" Mary asks.
> " 'The way to dusty death.' Robin hopes to play the First Murderer
> at the end of term."

Just as Victor is cheated of his Roman death by the incongruity
of heroics in the commonplace of his domestic life, so Ann Howard,
a teenage daughter of family friends who is infatuated with Clive
Root, is cheated of a romance with the older man. "You've read too
much Zane Grey," Mary tells her. "Clive isn't one of your great

open spaces. He's more like an over-crowded town. Only I happen
to love over-crowded towns . . . ." But Mary herself is frustrated of
freedom to enjoy her lover. Victor bumbles into their hotel bedroom; Robin chanting off-stage "Mother, Mother, Mother" is a
persistent domestic chorus; and Clive finally predicts that whatever
arrangements they make to continue their affair, he will eventually
"get tired of waiting outside shops in Paris or Brussels while you
buy the children's shoes." Clive too is prisoner of the prosaic. In
another generation his father, like Clive of India, had taken his
own life, but his own opportunity for heroism is limited to buying
Dutch currency on the black market, and when faced with failure
he agrees to the compromising solution of becoming a complaisant
lover.

By the agency of the commonplace Victor and the practical joke
in the end triumph. When he meets his rival alone in the closing
moments of the play, his dentistry, which has been a symbol of the
unromantic and the butt of many jokes, is used to key up his victory.

"Well? This interview had to come, hadn't it?" says Root grimly.
"Yes," says Victor crossing over to him. "Just stay where you are for
a moment. Now open your mouth. There's just something . . ."
and taking out a pocket flashlight he looks at Clive's teeth. "I'm
afraid you don't have a very good dentist." "What are you talking
about?" "That filling in the upper canine—it shows too much. Like
an old sardine tin . . . ." And surprised into concern Clive agrees
to telephone Victor's secretary and make an appointment.

From here on the situation is in Victor's hands. He rescues Clive
from the musical chair, pours him a drink of his best whiskey (no
dribbling glass), and persuades him, for Mary's sake, to enter into
a comic *ménage à trois,* to "let her have her cake and eat it too."
Then, accepting his own part in the practical joke of complaisancy
with kindly gravity, he puts the final test to Clive's sense of
humour. "Come to dinner on Thursday," he says. "No party. Just
the three of us." "Yes, please come," says Mary, "and in gratitude
to her husband she puts her arm around him." "Clive looks at the
married pair and sadly accepts his fate. 'Oh yes, I'll come,' he says
reluctantly. 'I expect I'll come.' "

The casual reader or spectator may first be struck by several
obvious carry-overs from Greene's more familiar melodramatic

manner. Although the play observes many of the conventions of drawing room comedy, it pushes perilously close to Greene's favorite tragic subject, suicide; its humour is what one might expect of a writer of melodrama turned to comedy, not only verging at times on the pathetic, but hinged on a grotesque comic device, the practical joke; and finally, the solution of "complaisancy" remains as disconcerting as any of the tragic enigmas which close the earlier novels.

But when one considers the compulsive nature of Greene's creative vision and how indelibly it marks everything he writes, his artistry in suppressing and controlling the melodramatic impulse in this play is the striking accomplishment. The point is not that he introduces suicide, but that he successfully skirts it; his use of the practical joke, for all its superficial grotesqueness, is complex and subtle; and the ending can just as well be interpreted in the new comic spirit as in the old spirit of insoluble tragic dilemma.

To begin with the last point: almost inevitably an audience will be inclined to reject Greene's ending and, if only subconsciously, to prefer a melodramatic and, if necessary, tragic alternative to complaisancy. The chief popular criticism of the play, so conspicuously anti-romantic in theme, is that plot and characterization are not realistic. No woman could be quite so prodigal, runs the conventional argument, and no man, either husband or lover, let alone both, could be quite so indulgent. Without arguing probability one can say that Greene stands in relation to such a critical and incredulous audience as the practical joker before his humourless victim. The conclusion *is* false, if you will—like the imitation cigar —and all one can justly complain of is smelling a plastic rat. The play comes emphatically to its artificial end in the figure of the complaisant triangle, just as Restoration comedy closes with the pat pairing of the final tableau. Yet the very artificiality of the conclusion is instructive. Had Greene wished, by other means, to force his modern audience into the compromising position of readily accepting a more tragic end, he could not have succeeded better. And this is the first indication that in this play Greene himself may be something less than the complacent playwright that he appears to be.

Greene's treatment of the practical joke is also revealing. In the first act Clive, who has just been taken in by the rubber cigar trick, comments wryly: "Jokes like this must be compensation for something. When we are children we're powerless, and these jokes make us feel superior to our dictators. But now we're grown up, there are no dictators . . . ." And elesewhere Greene writes of the hoax as being performed by "men who sympathize with the defeated and despize the conqueror and dare do nothing but trivial mischief to assert their independence." This is indeed the means by which Victor, at first unconsciously, asserts his independence in the face of conquering lover Clive Root. In the end it is his means of victory over what in terms of romance or melodrama would be a tragically insoluble solution. And interestingly enough, our sympathy swells for Clive in the measure that he progressively loses dictatorial power and becomes himself a failure as a conventional lover and a reluctant participant in the joke.

Furthermore the childishness that Clive at first criticizes in Victor's tricks is a quality which, through innuendo and oblique reference, is consistently developed and sanctioned throughout the play. Victor's jokes, tolerated with bad grace by the grown-ups, have the support of his children, especially Robin. The lovers' difficulties are echoed on a child's level in Robin's devotion to Ann Howard (Clive gives Mary diamond earrings, Robin gives Ann an electronic eye and a stuffed mouse), just as they are played out again on the adolescent level in Ann's infatuation with Clive Root. It is Mary who understands the essential similarity between these loves. "Give him a smile, Ann, when he comes in," she says. "The mouse meant a lot. I can never understand why people laugh at children's love. Love's painful at any age."

Mary's own love is perhaps the clearest example of the childlike impulse which Greene defends in this play. Like many earlier Greene heroines, and above all like Sarah in *The End of the Affair,* she is a mixture of innocence and experience, not worldly experience but a kind of childlike wisdom which gives her a direct perception of the facts of life. Mary, like Sarah, is recklessly prodigal in love once committed, and like a child simply accepts that loyalty to love is absolute and overrides any other law or social convention. When faced with a choice between her love for Victor and their children and her passion for Clive, she is incapable of refusing either.

"She wants to have her cake and eat it," says Clive. "That's exactly what she said," Victor replies. "Don't you love her enough to try to give her that kind of cake? A child's cake with silver balls and mauve icing and a layer of marzipan." "Bad for the teeth my nurse used to say." "Not for children's teeth," says dentist Victor.

Mary's attitude towards love triumphs in the end together with the practical joke. Both stem from the same childlike anarchy in outlook which will not accept conventional sanity and order, society's adult dictates, or the usual legal compromise. Both basically refuse the way of the world. It is a kind of perverse romanticism in a sense, this absurd hostility to the conventional. But it has been a constant in Greene's fiction where the question has repeatedly arisen: what if the world's way, the way of the institution, society, the law, were romantic and wrong, and what if the erratic way of the individual were right? And Greene's heroes—criminals, spies, outlaws, heretics and illicit lovers—have always stood alone against the world, relying not on social justice, but on love or divine mercy within the context of the novel, and on the sympathy of the reader in a larger context.

This defence of the individual against the opinion of the mass is so important to Greene that it is not only a central theme in his work but even his *raison d'être* as a writer. He goes so far as to praise "disloyalty" as the prime virtue of the creative writer. "If only writers could maintain that one virtue—so much more important to them than purity—unspotted from the world," he exclaims in *Why Do I Write?* "But the world knows only too well that given time the writer will be corrupted into loyalty . . . Loyalty confines us to accepted opinions, loyalty forbids us to comprehend sympathetically our dissident fellows; but disloyalty encourages us to roam experimentally through any human mind: it gives to the novelist the extra dimension of sympathy." From this point of view *The Complaisant Lover* fulfills the essential creative purpose, for it permits Greene, in his characterization of childlike Victor and irrational Mary, to side with the dissident by exercising the writer's extra faculty of sympathy.

The practical joke then, far from being simply the grotesque Greene equivalent of humour in *The Complaisant Lover,* is used for three important purposes. Technically Greene uses it to introduce something of that "seedy" quality familiar to readers of his earlier fiction. This seediness, equated to unheroic failure and fallibility in his characters, becomes one of the philosophical premises of the play. Thematically the joke is also designed to assert faith in a child's response to reality, Victor's, Mary's, and in the end Clive's. Finally it is an excellent vehicle for expressing Greene's purpose as a writer. With Greene as practical joker and the audience as victim, the joke of *The Complaisant Lover* is just another instance of that perennial challenge to authority which seems to be a necessary condition of his creative act.

Greene's final achievement in this play is to have shown a considerable gain in objectivity. Of course, the comic form requires this, but in large measure Greene has been able to provide it. Most of his earlier novels, and *The Living Room,* end with a provocative question debated by two groups of characters, one group representing justice, law, morality and conventional society, the other, Greene's favoured few, soliciting mercy, sympathy, indulgence and respect for the individual. Rather than close with a burning question—will Rose expiate for Pinkie?—is the Mexican priest saint or sinner?—is Scobie damned or saved?—Greene now commits himself to an answer. It is the function of the writer of comedy to furnish answers, to dispense justice, and in *The Complaisant Lover* Greene not only entangles his characters in a dilemma but dissolves their perplexities. At the end of the play he hears their repentance (the phrase "I'm sorry" occurs six times in different combinations in the last ten pages), and dispenses absolution. At the curtain his characters are not grouped in opposition but stand together: all three are complaisant, the joke is complete.

Notice that Greene's peculiar sense of justice, whose expression is the practical joke of complaisance, permits him to achieve a critical purpose which resounds beyond the conclusion of the play. His solution, while it satisfies the requirements of the comic form, remains challenging or impossible to a conventional public for it demands of them, no less than the conclusion of any of his serious novels, that they revise their stock ideas of justice and rely on a childish faith in love. It allows Greene to practise the writer's "virtue" of disloyalty and to perform what he calls "the genuine duty we (writers) owe society: to be a piece of grit in the state machinery." The joke which he leaves the public to swallow or choke on fulfills that function perfectly while comic author Greene sits back to have his cake and eat it too.

In final evaluation one might apply to this play those criteria which Greene himself set in the thirties for judging films and drama. *The Complaisant Lover* does meet Chekhov's double requirement of realism and criticism: it presents a mature view of life as it is, with its full quota of pain and unhappiness, yet it also presents a vision of life as it should be, and contains a strong element of satire. Criticism is no longer carried in the broad abstractions of Greene's earlier melodramatic fiction, but the play is still written out of the same obsessive convictions and still has the bones of a consistent moral outlook.

It is true that Greene seems to have abandoned his early ideal of "a genuinely vulgar art . . . as popular and unsubtle as a dance tune." *The Complaisant Lover* is "class entertainment" written for a restricted, well-to-do, West End or Broadway audience, and it must be admitted that the world of adultery and assignations in Amsterdam is a pretty specialized one. The saving grace is that Greene remains uncomplacent. He does not compromise with this world but challenges it with a solution which borders on vulgarity. In the eyes of modern conventionality he remains a boor and a disloyal bohemian to the last.

It must be said, however, that in the shift from the popular, melodramatic macrocosm to the bourgeois, domestic microcosm, and from a tragic to a comic vision, Greene has sacrificed some of his original vitality. And despite the technical skill of *The Complaisant Lover* his play shows the signs of strain that might be expected from the discipline of submitting a personal, obsessive, and naturally religious outlook to the objective, conservative, and essentially irreligious standards of contemporary comedy. Whereas the novel makes a private appeal, drama is a public art, and Greene has accepted the challenge of translating his point of view into the language and conventions of the modern stage. That he has met it so well is the best promise that one day he may feel free enough in the form to write the type of popular, universal drama to which he aspired in his youth and recognized in the plays of Jonson and Shakespeare; that he may outgrow the comedy of the practical joke and achieve something of their breadth of comic vision.

What path must this development take? Greene himself analysed Shakespeare's greatness as his ability to maintain "perfect dialectical tension" between the morality and the play of character. This is very close to Chekhov's balancing a sense of life as it is and a sense of life as it ought to be. But the comic vision is rather concerned to balance a *love* of life as it is with a sense of life as it should be. It is this love of life, "the sense of huge enjoyment" which Greene disengages as the predominant quality in Jonson's plays. And indeed it is the obvious relish with which Jonson enters into the excesses of Sir Epicure Mammon or Volpone that assures the success of his comic characterization. The range of Greene's own creative sympathy is not yet so large. He lacks Jonson's double capacity to love the world for itself while at the same time ridiculing its imperfections.

Not only has Greene been unable to accept the world but, more introspective, he has also found it difficult to accept and forget himself. He has shown us vividly in his novels and plays that to create character imaginatively is an act of self-humiliation, is to identify oneself with the dissident, with the guilty as well as the innocent, with the smug and complacent as well as with the shabby and the dull. But there is a considerable margin between self-humiliation and humility, and so far Greene has been incapable of following Jonson or Shakespeare in the complete submergence of himself in his material and in the sacrifice of personal obsessions to the demands of his subject; in that act of artistic humility which guarantees the final comprehensiveness of the comic vision.

That he has made remarkable progress in all these respects over the last ten years, however, is shown both in *The Complaisant Lover* and in that brilliant tragi-comic novel *A Burnt-Out Case*. If he follows his bent and continues to experiment in the drama we can expect of him more sadly funny plays, entertaining and provocative at the same time. But perhaps he will not follow his bent, perhaps he will manage to be disloyal to himself and pursue the artistic challenge of working almost against the grain in a new medium. Perhaps he will give us a really great comic novel or play, for he has passed what Evelyn Waugh calls "the dangerous climacteric where so many talents fail," and he is one of the very few English writers today who has the capacity and compulsion to renew himself, even though he already has to his credit an outstanding and original achievement in a different manner and genre.

The Art of Fiction: Graham Greene

by Martin Shuttleworth and Simon Raven

In the interview held with Graham Greene in the spring of 1953, the author constantly reminded the interviewers that the key to his craft was to be found among the works themselves. Thus the following quotations are offered. They are removed from their contexts and occasionally the process has entailed a change of tense, person or article.

> *Every creative writer worth our consideration, every writer who can be called in the wide eighteenth century use of the term a poet, is a victim: a man given over to an obsession.*

> *Gaugin's great phrase: "Life being what it is one dreams of revenge."*

> *The creative writer perceives his world once and for all in childhood and adolescence, and his whole career is an effort to illustrate his private world in terms of the great public world we all share.*

> *With the death of James the religious sense was lost to the English novel.*

> *How tired we have become of the pure novel, the tradition founded by Flaubert and reaching its magnificent tortuous climax in England in the works of Henry James.*

> *When—perhaps I was fourteen at the time—I took Miss Marjorie Bowen's* The Viper of Milan *from the library shelf, the future for better or worse really struck. From that moment I began to write . . . Why? On the surface* The Viper of Milan *is only the story of a war between Gian Galeazzo Visconti, Duke of Milan, and Mastino della Scala, Duke of Verona, told with zest and cunning and an*

amazing pictorial sense. Why did it creep and color and explain the
terrible living world of the stone stairs and the never quiet dormi-
tory? . . . As for Visconti, with his beauty, his patience and his
genius for evil, I had watched him pass by many a time in his black
Sunday suit smelling of mothballs. His name was Carter. He ex-
ercised terror from a distance like a snowcloud over the young fields.
Goodness has only once found a perfect incarnation in a human
body and never will again, but evil can always find a home there.
Human nature is not black and white but black and grey. I read
all that in The Viper of Milan *and I looked round and saw that it*
was so.

And finally, a selection from Æ (George Russell) which Greene
considers among his favorite lines of verse:

> *In ancient shadows and twilights*
> *Where childhood had strayed,*
> *The world's great sorrows were born*
> *And its heroes were made.*
> *In the lost boyhood of Judas*
> *Christ was betrayed.*

Scene

The eighteenth century succeeds to the twentieth on the ground
floors at the bottom of St. James's Street. The gloss and the cello-
phane of oyster bars and travel agencies are wrapped incongruously
round the legs of the dignified houses. Graham Greene lives here at
the commercial end of this thoroughfare in a flat on the first floor
of a narrow house sandwiched between the clubs of the aristocracy
and St. James's Palace. Above him, General Auchinleck, the soldier
who was beaten by Rommel; below him, the smartest oyster bar in
Europe; opposite the second smartest.

Readers of *Cakes and Ale* will remember that it was near here that
Maugham met Hugh Walpole, but it is not the sort of area in
which one expects to find a novelist, even a successful novelist. It's
an area black with smartness, the Rolls-Royces and the bowler
hats of the men are black, the court shoes and the correct suits of
the women are black and in the most august flats even the bathing
pools set into the floors of the bathrooms are paved with black
marble. Nearby are the courtyard and sundial of Pickering Place

where only the very rich penetrate to eat and wine in Carolinean isolation.

Isolation, the isolation of anonymity rather than that of wealth, is probably the lure for Greene, for he is, or was until recently, a man shy of the contacts that congeal to fame. Brown suited, brown shoed, browned face, he opened the door when we rang and ushered us up above the oyster bar to the large room. It was cold for April and a large number of electric fires were burning in various corners of the room. A many-lamped standard of Scandinavian design stood by the window; a couple of bulbs were lit, they made as much difference to the watery April light as a pair of afterburners to a flagging jet engine. They revealed a book-lined room with a desk, a dictaphone and a typewriter; great padded armchairs and a furry rug. A painting by Jack Yeats overstood the mantle; sombre, Celtic, yet delicate, it had something in common with the red pastel drawings by Henry Moore whose sad classicism against the wall was in keeping with the brownness that dominated the whole room. Brown as the headmaster's study or the little office in Lagos where he once said he might willingly have spent forty dreary years, brown as his collection of books was blue—blue with the blueness that the bindings of English academic publishers give to the shelves and studies of dons and scholarly men of letters. It was a shock; subconsciously we had expected black and purple of a Catholic bookshop; a violence to match Mexico, Brighton and West Africa—what we had found was a snuggery, a den such as might be found in any vicarage or small country house in England. The only suggestion of an obsession, or of anything out of the ordinary (for so many people have Henry Moores these days) was a collection of seventy-four different miniature whiskey bottles, ranged on top of a bookcase, bizarre as an international convention of Salesian novices.

In the retreat of the man within the novelist, the man whom we had come to besiege, they were a welcome discovery.

INTERVIEWERS: Mr. Greene, we thought that we could make the best use of our time here if we brought along a few focal questions and let the conversation eddy round them. We felt that any formal questionnaire which we might make out would be based only on a knowledge of your written work and that a portion of the answers would be contained in the assumptions that allowed us to formulate the questions; we wanted to get beyond this and so we have come prepared to let the conversation lead us and to try to find out, so far as you will let us, the unknown things about you.

GREENE: *Very frank. What will you have to drink?* (He produced a bottle and brought water in a majolica jug.)

INTERVIEWERS: Shall we begin by working backwards from your latest production, your play *The Living Room*. It has not been seen in America yet so you will excuse us if we go into it in some detail.

GREENE: *Have you seen this play yourselves?*

INTERVIEWERS: No, a percipient girl saw it for us—she went down to Portsmouth and came back with a review, a synopsis and a great admiration for it.

GREENE: *I am glad; it's my first play. I've been a film man to date and I was rather afraid that I had written it in such filmic terms that it might not have succeeded as a play.*

INTERVIEWERS: She enjoyed it well enough. She felt that you had conveyed the tense, haunted atmosphere of a house in which a family was decaying because of its ill-conceived gentility and religion; that you had made a drama out of the situation of the girl who was lost in the desert between the unhappiness, truth and family that lay in the background and the lover and mirage of happiness that lay in the foreground. Her main criticism, and this perhaps has something to do with what you were saying just now about the difference between film and theatrical technique, was that you had made the drama depend too much on dialogue and not enough on action.

GREENE: *There I disagree. I obeyed the unities. I confined myself to one set and I made my characters act, one upon the other. What other sort of action can you have? I get fed up with all this nonsense of ringing people up and lighting cigarettes and answering the doorbell that passes for action in so many modern plays. No, what I meant about filmic terms was that I was so used to the dissolve that I had forgotten about the curtain and so used to the camera, which is only turned on when it is wanted, that I had forgotten that actors and actresses are on the stage all the time and I had left out many functional lines. Still most of that has been put right now.*

INTERVIEWERS: Then the criticism, if it stands, means that the dialogue fell short in some other way; perhaps it was too closely related to the dialogue of your novels which doesn't often carry the burden of the action.

GREENE: *I think that is nearer the mark: I tried to fuse everything and put it into the dialogue but I did not quite succeed.* (With a smile) *I will next time.*

INTERVIEWERS: The particular thing which impressed this critic of ours was your attitude towards the girl's suicide. This is what she writes: "The central point of much of Greene's writing has been suicide, in Catholic doctrine the most deadly sin. But in this play at least his interpretation of it is not a doctrinal one. We are left quite definitely feeling that her soul is saved, if anyone's is, and the message of the play, for it does not pretend not to have a message, is not mere Catholic propaganda but of far wider appeal. It is a plea to believe in a God who Father Browne, the girl's confessor, admits may not exist, but belief can only do good not ill and without it we cannot help ourselves . . . the girl's suicide will probable be the only answer visible to most people but Father Browne's own unshaken faith, his calm acceptance of her death, implies that there is another, but that the struggle for it must be unceasing."

GREENE: *Yes I would say that that is roughly true but the message is still Catholic.*

INTERVIEWERS: How do you make that out?

GREENE: *The church is compassionate you know . . .*

INTERVIEWERS: Sorry to interrupt you but could we ask a correlative question now to save going back later?

GREENE: *Go ahead.*

INTERVIEWERS: Scobie in *The Heart of the Matter* committed suicide too. Was it your purpose when you wrote *The Living Room* to show a similar predicament and to show that suicide in certain circumstances can almost amount to an act of redemption?

GREENE: *Steady, steady. Let's put it this way. I write about situations that are common, universal might be more correct, in which my characters are involved and from which only faith can redeem them, though often the actual manner of the redemption is not immediately clear. They sin, but there is no limit to God's mercy and because this is important, there is a difference between not confessing in fact and the complacent and the pious may not realize it.*

INTERVIEWERS: In this sense Scobie, Rose (the girl in *The Living Room*), the boy Pinkie in *Brighton Rock* and the whiskey priest of *The Power and the Glory* are all redeemed?

GREENE: *Yes, though redemption is not the exact word. We must be careful of our language. They have all understood in the end. This is perhaps the religious sense.*

INTERVIEWERS: So we have touched the nerve of the theme, the theme that gives, as you have said somewhere yourself, to a shelf of novels the unity of a system?

GREENE: *Yes, or rather it explains the unity of a group of my novels which is now, I think, finished.*

INTERVIEWERS: Which group?

GREENE: Brighton Rock, The Power and the Glory, The Heart of the Matter, *and* The End of the Affair. *My next novel will not deal explicitly with Catholic themes at all.*

INTERVIEWERS: So the *New Statesman* gibe that *The End of the Affair* is the last novel which a layman will be able to read is about to be disproved?

GREENE: *Yes, I think so, as far as one can tell oneself. I think that I know what the next novel is about but one never really knows, of course, until it's finished.*

INTERVIEWERS: Was that so of the earlier books?

GREENE: *The very earliest ones particularly* . . .

INTERVIEWERS: Yes, what about them? How did you find their subjects? Their historical romanticism is so different from what came later, even from the Entertainments.

GREENE: *How does one find one's subjects?—gradually I suppose. My first three*—The Man Within, The Name of Action, Rumour at Nightfall—*as far as one is influenced by anybody and I don't think that one is consciously influenced, were influenced by Stevenson and Conrad and they are what they are because at the time those were the subjects that I wanted to write about. The Entertainments* (Stamboul Train, *written a year after* Rumour at Nightfall *is the first of them; then* Gun for Sale, The Confidential Agent, The Ministry of Fear, *and* The Third Man *and* The Fallen Idol) *are distinct from the novels because as the name implies they do not carry a message (horrible word).*

INTERVIEWERS: They show traces though of the same obsession; they are written from the same point of view . . .

GREENE: *Yes, I wrote them. They are not all that different.*

INTERVIEWERS: There is a great break between *Rumour at Nightfall* and *England Made Me* (our favorite novel of yours). What caused the historical novelist to turn into the contemporary one?

GREENE: *I have a particularly soft spot for* England Made Me, *too. The book came about when I began* Stamboul Train. *I had to write a pot-boiler, a modern adventure story, and I suddenly discovered that I liked the form, that the writing came easily, that I was beginning to find my world. In* England Made Me *I let myself go in it for the first time.*

INTERVIEWERS: You had begun to read James and Mauriac?

GREENE: *Yes, I had begun to change. I had found that what I wanted to express, my fixations if you like, could best be expressed in the melodramatic, the contemporary and later the Catholic novel.*

INTERVIEWERS: What influence has Mauriac had over you?

GREENE: *Again very little I think.*

INTERVIEWERS: But you told Kenneth Allott, who quotes it in his book about you, that Mauriac had a distinct influence.

GREENE: *Did I? That is the sort of thing that one says under pressure. I read* Thérèse *in 1930 and was turned up inside but, as I have said, I don't think that he had any influence on me unless it was an unconscious one. Our Catholicism is very different: I don't see the resemblance that people talk about.*

INTERVIEWERS: Where do the differences in your Catholicism lie?

GREENE: *Mauriac's sinners sin against God whereas mine, however hard they try, can never quite manage to* . . . (His voice fell.)

INTERVIEWERS: Then Mauriac is almost a Manichee whereas you . . . . (*The telephone rang and when, after a brief conversation, Greene came back to his long low seat between the electric fires and topped up the glasses, the conversation was not resumed, for the point, we thought, if not implied, was difficult for him to discuss.*)

INTERVIEWERS: Can we now discuss this fresh period that you mentioned just now?

GREENE: *We can but I don't think that you'll find out much, for it has not begun yet. All that I can tell you is that I do know that my next novel is to be about an entirely different set of people with entirely different roots.*

INTERVIEWERS: Perhaps then it would be more profitable to talk about the roots of your previous sets of characters? If we leave the historical romantic novels and the Entertainments out of it for the moment and concentrate on the contemporary ones it is obvious that there is a relationship between the characters which is a product in part of your absorption with failure, pursuit and poverty, and in part with interest in a particular type of person.

GREENE: *I agree with you, of course, when you say that there is a relationship between, let us say, Anthony Farrant in* England

Made Me *and Pinkie, or Scobie, even—but they are not the same sort of person even if they are the expressions of what critics are pleased to call my fixations. I don't know exactly where they came from but I think that I have now got rid of them.*

INTERVIEWERS: Ah, now, these fixations—they are what really matter, aren't they? We don't quite understand why you consider that it is so important for a novelist to be dominated in this way.

GREENE: *Because if he is not he has to rely on his talent, and talent, even of a very high order, cannot sustain an achievement, whereas a ruling passion gives, as I have said, to a shelf of novels the unity of a system.*

INTERVIEWERS: Mr. Greene, if a novelist did not have this ruling passion, might it be possible to fabricate it?

GREENE: *How do you mean?*

INTERVIEWERS: Well, put it this way and I hope we won't seem to be impertinent: the contrast between the Nelson Places and the Mexicos of the novels and this flat in St. James's is marked. Urbanity, not tragedy, seems to reign in this room. Do you find, in your own life, that it is difficult to live at the high pitch of perception that you require of your characters?

GREENE: *Well this is rather difficult to answer. Could you perhaps qualify the question a bit?*

INTERVIEWERS: You made Scobie say in *The Heart of the Matter*: *Point me out the happy man and I will show you either egotism, selfishness, evil or else an absolute ignorance.* What worries us is that you yourself seem to be so much happier than we had expected. Perhaps we are being rather naive but the seventy-four miniature whiskey bottles, the expression on your face, so different from the fixed set look of your photograph, the whole atmosphere, seem to be the products of something much more positive than that very limited optimum of happiness that you described in *The Power and the Glory* in this passage: *the world is all much of a piece: it is engaged everywhere in the same sub-terranean struggle . . . there is no peace anywhere where there is life; but there are quiet and active sectors of the line.*

GREENE: (With a smile) *Oh yes, I see what troubles you. I think that you have misjudged me and my consistency. This flat, my way of life—these are simply my hole in the ground.*

INTERVIEWERS: A moderately comfortable hole.

GREENE: *Shall we leave it at that?*

INTERVIEWERS: Of course. There are just one or two other questions on a similar tack: many of your most memorable characters, Raven for instance, are from low life. Have you ever had any experience of low life?

GREENE: *No, very little.*

INTERVIEWERS: What did you know about poverty?

GREENE: *I have never known it. I was "short," yes, in the sense that I had to be careful for the first eight years of my adult life but I have never been any closer.*

INTERVIEWERS: Then you don't draw your characters from life?

GREENE: *No, one never knows enough about characters in real life to put them into novels. One gets started and then, suddenly, one can not remember what toothpaste they use: what are their views on interior decoration, and one is stuck utterly. No, major characters emerge: minor ones may be photographed.*

INTERVIEWERS: Well now, how do you work? Do you work at regular hours?

GREENE: *I used to; now I set myself a number of words.*

INTERVIEWERS: How many?

GREENE: *Five hundred, stepped up to seven fifty as the book gets on. I re-read the same day, again the next morning and again and again until the passage has got too far behind to matter to the bit that I am writing. Correct in type, final correction in proof.*

INTERVIEWERS: Do you correct much?

GREENE: *Not over-much.*

INTERVIEWERS: Did you always want to be a writer?

GREENE: *No, I wanted to be a businessman and all sorts of other things; I wanted to prove to myself that I could do something else.*

INTERVIEWERS: Then the thing that you could always do was write?

GREENE: *Yes, I suppose it was.*

INTERVIEWERS: What happened to your business career?

GREENE: *Initially it lasted for a fortnight. They were a firm, I remember, of tobacco merchants. I was to go up to Leeds to learn the business and then go abroad. I couldn't stand my companion. He was an insufferable bore. We would play double noughts and crosses and he always won. What finally got me was when he said: "We'll be able to play this on the way out, won't we?" I resigned immediately.*

INTERVIEWERS: Then you became a journalist?

GREENE: *Yes, for the same reason—that I wanted to prove I could do something else.*

INTERVIEWERS: But after *The Man Within* you gave it up?

GREENE: *Then I became a professional author.*

INTERVIEWERS: So that is what you meant when you said "I am an author who is a Catholic?"

GREENE: *Indeed it is. I don't believe that anyone had ever realized that I was a Catholic until 1938 when I began to review for* The Tablet *and, for fun, or rather to give system to a series of reviews of unrelated books, I started to review from a Catholic standpoint. If it had not been for that . . .*

INTERVIEWERS: But surely a person would have to be very obtuse who reads any novel from *Brighton Rock* onwards and does not realize it?

GREENE: *Some people still manage to. In fact, a Dutch priest wrote to me the other day, discussing* The Power and the Glory, *and concluded his letter: "Well I suppose that even if you aren't a Catholic, you are not too hostile to us."*

INTERVIEWERS: Oh well, internal criticism.

GREENE: *All the same you see what I mean.*

INTERVIEWERS: Yes, you are "a writer who is a Catholic," we seem to have cleared up that, but there are still a few gaps to be filled before we can know why you are a writer. Do you remember that you once said on the wireless that when you were fourteen or so and read Marjorie Bowen's *Viper of Milan* you immediately began to scribble imitation after imitation: *from that moment I began to write. All the other possible futures slid away . . .*

GREENE: *Yes, that was so, I am very grateful to Marjorie Bowen. In that talk I was engaged on a little mild baiting of the intellectuals. Pritchett had said that Turgenev had influenced him most; somebody else, somebody else. I chose Marjorie Bowen because as I have told you, I don't think that the books that one reads as an adult influence one as a writer. For example, of the many many books on the art of the novel, only Percy Lubbock's* The Craft of Fiction *has interested me at all. But books such as Marjorie Bowen's read at a young age do influence one considerably. It is a very fine book you know. I re-read it again recently.*

INTERVIEWERS: We haven't read it but from your description in the broadcast (*reprinted at the front of this interview*) it seems that the book has many features in common with your writing as well as with your philosophy. You said that *The Viper of Milan* gave you your pattern of life: *that religion later might explain it to me in other terms, but the pattern was already there—perfect evil walking the world where perfect good can never walk again, and only the pendulum ensures that after all in the end justice is done.* That explains a great deal about your philosophy and it seems that the heightened colors and the violence of the Renaissance, as it is depicted by Miss Bowen and also as it is shown in the plays of Webster, also have their counterpart in your writing. As Edwin Muir has said of you: "Everything is shown up in a harsh light and casts fantastic colors."

GREENE: *Yes, there is a lot to that. It is true, to a certain extent, about the earlier books but I don't think that it does justice to the later ones, for melodrama is one of my working tools and it enables me to obtain effects that would be unobtainable other-*

wise, but on the other hand I am not deliberately melodramatic; don't get too annoyed if I say that I write in the way that I do because I am what I am.

INTERVIEWERS: Do you ever need the stimulus of drink to write?

GREENE: *No, on the contrary, I can only write when I am absolutely sober.*

INTERVIEWERS: Do you find collaboration easy, in particular collaboration with directors and producers?

GREENE: *Well, I have been exceptionally lucky both with Carol Reed and recently with Peter Glanvill. I like film work, even the impersonality of it. I have managed to retain a certain amount of control over my own stories so I have not suffered as badly as some people seem to have; all the same, film-making can be a distressing business for, when all is said and done, a writer's part in making a film is relatively small.*

INTERVIEWERS: Did it take you long to learn?

GREENE: *I learnt a lot on some not very good films before the war so I was into my stride by the time that* The Fallen Idol *and* The Third Man *came along.*

INTERVIEWERS: Do you see much of your fellow authors?

GREENE: *Not much, they are not one's material. A few of them are very dear friends of mine but for a writer to spend much of his time in the company of authors is, you know, a form of masturbation.*

INTERVIEWERS: What was the nature of your friendship with Norman Douglas?

GREENE: *We were so different that we could be friends. He was very tolerant in his last years and if he thought me odd he never said so.*

INTERVIEWERS: Is there, in fact, any relationship between his paganism and your Catholicism?

GREENE: *Not really, but his work, for which I have the very greatest admiration, was so remote from mine that I was able to enjoy*

*it completely; to me it was like a great block of stone, which
not being a sculptor myself, I had no temptation to tamper with,
yet could admire wholeheartedly for its beauty and strength.*

INTERVIEWERS: Yes, of course, there couldn't be any real connection
between your writing and his—or between yours and Mauriac's.
For as you have said, your sinners can never sin against God no
matter how hard they try but . . .

*(The telephone rang. Mr. Greene smiled in a faint deprecatory
way as if to signify he'd said all he wished to say, picked up the
instrument and spoke into it.)*

GREENE: *Hello? Hello Peter! How is Andrea? Oh, it's the other
Peter. How is Maria? No, I can't do it this evening. I've got
Mario Soldati on my hands—we're doing a film in Italy this
summer. I'm co-producing. How about Sunday? Battersea? Oh,
they're not open? Well, then, we'll go to my pleasant little Negro
night club round the corner. . . .*

Graham Greene: On the Screen

by Gene D. Phillips

In reviewing Graham Greene's *The Heart of the Matter*, Evelyn Waugh described Greene's narrative style this way: "It is as though, out of an infinite length of film, sequences had been cut which, assembled, comprise an experience which is the reader's alone, without any correspondence to the experience of the protagonists. The writer has become director and producer. Indeed, the affinity of the film is everywhere apparent. It is the camera's eye which . . . moves about the room . . . recording significant detail. It is the modern way of telling a story. Now it is the cinema which has taught a new habit of narrative."

And Roger Sharrock has written more recently, "Long before they were made into film scripts his narratives were crisply cut like cinema montage." In addition to employing a cinematic narrative style, Graham Greene has written film criticism and scripted films, usually adaptations of his own fiction. His film criticism, some of the best of our age, according to Sharrock, appeared between 1935 and 1939 in *The Spectator* and in the short-lived *Night and Day*, of which Greene was co-editor in 1937.

Almost all of his fiction has been translated to the screen but the script has usually been by another hand, and in most cases it has been proven over and over again that no one except Greene himself can transfer his vivid prose into visual images and still retain his multiple levels of meaning. Deborah Kerr told me, concerning the film version of *The End of the Affair* for which Greene did not do the script: "I loved the film and believed in it, even though it was not a great success. It was almost impossible to bring across on the screen the changes in the woman that were taking place, as

"Graham Greene: On the Screen," by Gene D. Phillips. From *The Catholic World*, 209 (August 1969), 218–21. Copyright © 1969 by *The Catholic World*. Reprinted by permission of the publisher.

Mr. Greene was able to do in the novel. I believed that a woman could change and be willing to sacrifice her lover for a higher motive and played it that way, but this was difficult to convey in the film."

Graham Greene is one of the first major literary talents of our time to have shown serious interest in the motion picture medium. Consequently, it was about his interest in the screen as well as in writing fiction that I questioned him when we met in his home in France.

When did you become interested in the cinema?

At Oxford, in the days of silent films. There was a review, long since defunct, called Close-Up *which dealt with all the major directors of the time. [He showed me a bound volume.] Besides writing film criticism in the 1930's, I did two film scripts around 1937. One of them,* The Green Cockatoo, *was terrible.*

In 1938 you contributed an article to a collection of essays called *Footnotes to the Film,* in which you said: "The cinema has got to appeal to millions; we have got to accept its popularity as a virtue, not turn away from it as a vice. The novelist may write for a few thousand readers, but the film artist must work for millions." You added in 1939 in your column in *The Spectator*: "A film with a severely limited appeal must be—to that extent— a bad film."

I think I should stand by that. By limited appeal, I mean a flop. A good film is seldom a complete flop. Whereas a book can be very good and still be a flop.

Do you agree with those of your critics who feel that your narrative style has been affected by your script writing for the screen?

I don't think my style as a writer has been influenced by my work for the cinema. My style has been influenced by my going to the cinema. It's a Battlefield was intentionally based on film technique, and it was written before I did any film scripts. It is my only deliberate attempt to tell a story in cinematic terms, and it is one of the few novels which I have written that has never been filmed.

In your preface to *Three Plays by Graham Greene* you describe the scriptwriter as a "forgotten man" once a film goes into production: "When the lines are at last spoken on the studio-floor" the scriptwriter "is not there to criticize and alter. . . . My own experience with screenwriting has been fortunate and happy, and yet with what relief I have gone back afterwards to the one-man business, to the privacy of a room in which I bear the full responsibility for failure."

Film is not mainly dialogue as is a stage play. It is impossible for the scriptwriter to have the technical knowledge to control the filming of his script. This is a fact, not a complaint. I have been fortunate in my work for the screen. My scripts have not often been altered. I haven't suffered much in that way.

You have written the script for five of your own stories: *Brighton Rock* (1947), *The Fallen Idol* (1948), *The Third Man* (1949), *Our Man in Havana* (1959), and *The Comedians* (1967). How did you proceed in making your adaptations of these works for the screen?

My approach is to write a treatment of the story which is then turned into a script. I cannot write the kind of treatment that is in the historical present. I write the treatment like a novel. What today is known as the novel of The Third Man *was really the treatment which I did before writing the script. That is why I say in the preface to the published version that it was not written to be read, but only to be seen.*

What is your favorite among the scripts which you have done?

The Fallen Idol *is my favorite screen work because it is more a writer's film than a director's.* The Third Man, *though it was more popular because of the song, "The Third Man Theme," is mostly action with only sketched characters. It was fun doing, but there is more of the writer in* The Fallen Idol.

In some of the screen versions of your fiction the ending of the story has been significantly altered. For example, *Brighton Rock* (which was called *Young Scarface* in the U.S.): after the death of the gangster Pinkie, Rose goes home to play the record which he made for her at the amusement park. She thinks that it will be a declaration of his love for her but the reader knows that it is a declaration of hatred. In the film the needle of the phonograph sticks and the camera pans up to a crucifix. Did your collaborator on the screenplay, Terrence Rattigan, provide this ending?

Terrence Rattigan wrote a treatment of a few pages with quite a different ending which was not used; the script was not really a collaboration. I liked the ending of the film and I am completely guilty. I have complete justification for the needle sticking on the gramophone record: I knew the distributors would not accept the ghastly ending of the book. I also knew that thinking people would realize that one day Rose would play the record and move the needle beyond the crack and thus get the shock with which the book ends. The ghastly outcome was only delayed. It was the director's idea to pan up to the crucifix on the wall. This gave the impression that the needle stuck miraculously. Earlier in the film Pinkie had tried to destroy the record but was interrupted by Rose. This explains the crack in the record; there is nothing miraculous about it.

Do you retain much of your original dialogue when you adapt your own fiction to the screen?

I use actual dialogue from the novel when it seems to fit. Often in the first version of the script a great deal of the original dialogue is kept. But it is slowly whittled away, in order to reduce the dialogue as much as possible. What has the right rhythm in the book because of the surrounding paragraphs may seem unreal on the screen and must be modified. Dialogue in fiction must have the appearance of reality, without having to be real, while on the screen the camera emphasizes the reality of the situation: you have to be closer in a film to real-life conversation in order that the dialogue will match the realistic settings.

TV critic Jack Gould wrote of the 1967 Laurence Olivier version of *The Power and the Glory* (which was released in Europe as a commercial film) that the "omission of the climax of Mr. Greene's novel—the arrival of the new priest to replace the cleric who had just perished before the firing squad—was especially unfortunate." Although John Ford's 1947 film of the same novel, called *The Fugitive,* departed greatly from the book, that film did at least have the shadow of the new priest falling across the doorway.

More than the shadow of the priest should be there. It is important to have the dialogue of the new priest with the child to show the change of mind in the child toward the dead priest, whom he did not respect until his death, and also to indicate that the Church goes on.

Father John Burke, the technical adviser for the film of *The Heart of the Matter* (1953) has told me that against his advice the suicide of the policeman Major Scobie was greatly obscured in the film's ending because the film makers thought Catholics would object to a Catholic taking his own life. Instead Scobie is killed trying to break up a street brawl.

I tried to persuade the company to leave it in. Trevor Howard, who played Scobie, and who is an intelligent actor, said he would do a re-take of the ending without charge. I even figured out a way of doing it without Trevor Howard: I wanted to show Scobie writing a suicide note with the gun at hand, thus making it clear that he intended to take his own life. At that moment he would be called away to the police action and be killed, apparently with the intention of suicide in his mind. I disclaim the ending of the film as it is. At any rate, I do not like the novel, and have never re-read it.

I have often wondered why films like *The Heart of the Matter,* which include peculiarly Catholic concepts like the sacrilegious reception of Holy Communion, appeal to the large non-Catholic audience.

For the same reason that they seem to buy the books on which the films are based. Any author writing strictly for a Catholic audience would not reach a large public. It goes back to what I said in the Footnotes to the Film *essay which you mentioned earlier: if you excite your audience first, you can put over what you will of horror, suffering, truth. This is still true and applies to the novel as well as to the film. By exciting the audience I mean getting them involved in the story. Once they are involved they will accept the thing as you present it.*

You once were quoted as saying, with reference to the controversy over the meaning of *The Heart of the Matter*: "I wrote a book about a man who goes to hell—*Brighton Rock*—another about a man who goes to heaven—*The Power and the Glory*. Now I have simply written one about a man who goes to purgatory. I don't know what all the fuss is about."

What I really meant was that, for example, Brighton Rock *is written in such a way that people could plausibly imagine that Pinkie went to hell, and then I cast doubt upon it in the ending. The real theme of the three novels is embodied in the priest's phrase at the end of* Brighton Rock: "*You can't conceive, my child, nor can anyone, the . . . appalling strangeness of the mercy of God.*"

Would you say that the period of your Catholic novels is over?

For one period I did write on Catholic subjects: from Brighton Rock *to* A Burnt-Out Case. *But the majority of my novels do not deal with Catholic themes. One only began with a Catholic subject because one found it a great interest of the moment. The* Comedians, *for example, is not a Catholic novel. Brown happens to be a Catholic; it was this formation that made him the type of person he was. But Brown, as I said in the preface, is not Greene. The* Comedians *is essentially a political novel. My period of Catholic novels was preceded and followed by political novels. It's a Battlefield and England Made Me were political novels. I was finding my way. Even the early thrillers were political:* The Confidential Agent *deals with the Spanish Civil War.* The Quiet American *and* The Comedians *are political novels. One has come full circle in a way. I am not taking back anything from my Catholic novels. The fact that Brown seems to continue in disbelief at the end of* The Comedians *should not be thought to mean that.*

Didn't *A Burnt-Out Case* explore both belief and unbelief? Incidentally, that is one of the few novels which you have written that was never filmed.

Plans to film that novel were abandoned when we could not get the director and the cast that we wanted. In A Burnt-Out Case *I wanted to show various grades of belief and disbelief. The hero's faith was lost temporarily and came back. There was a fanatical believer in the novel; a good believer, the superior of the mission, who was too busy to concern himself with doubt; and the doctor, who had a real belief in his atheism.*

To get back to *The Comedians,* how did you conceive that the screenplay should be written?

For purposes of the screen I had to leave out Brown's whole past. Beginning with the present, without the past, he would not have any character. But slowly, bit by bit, I brought out different sides of his character and developed them in the dialogue. My big problem when adapting one of my novels for the screen is that the kind of book I write, from the single point of view of one character, cannot be done the same way on the screen. You cannot look through the eyes of one character in a film. The novel was told from Brown's point of view. Brown remains the character who is on the screen more than any of the others. His comments on others are often there. But we still do not see others completely from his point of view as we do in the novel. For example, Martha's husband is despised by Brown in the book, but on the screen he is seen by others as a noble character.

Once again, the ending of the film differs from that of the book.

Brown is a beachcomber-type character. He had been washed up on the beach in Haiti. He is a person who could not be better than he is, although he would like to. At the end of the novel, which is black comedy, he becomes an undertaker: he is just washed up on another shore. In the film the ending is different but the point is the same. Brown is forced to join the guerrillas in the hills because he cannot return to Port-au-Prince. He does not want to go and he has no experience in guerrilla warfare, but he makes the best of the situation. I would not know what the future of Brown or of any of my characters would be at the end of one of my stories, however.

Since the title story of your most recent volume of short stories, *May We Borrow Your Husband?* is being filmed, I am reminded of a review of the book in which a British critic raised once again the old charge of Jansenism in your work, referring to what he called your habit of damning or exulting characters "in either case for capricious, Jansenist reasons."

People who think they are getting at Jansenism in my novels usually do not know what Jansenism really means. They probably mean Manichaeism. This is because in the Catholic novels I seem to believe in a supernatural evil. One gets so tired of people saying that my novels are about the opposition of Good and Evil. They are not about Good and Evil, but about human beings. After Hitler and Vietnam, one would have thought good and evil in people was more understandable. Still, I do not wish to judge any of my characters. I would hope it was common to most of us to have sympathy for the unfortunate part of the ordinary human character. As I once told another interviewer, I'm not a religious man, though it interests me. Religion is important, as atomic science is.

Even though your fiction has turned more toward politics than religion, will religion continue to be an important element in your work?

Space hasn't influenced my views of religion. I don't look for God up there, do you? He's not up there. He's down around here.

Chronology of Important Dates

1904   Greene born, October 2, at Berkhamsted, Hertfordshire.

1922–25   At Balliol College, Oxford.

1925   *Babbling April* (verse).

1925–26   Reporter, *Nottingham Journal.*

1926   Received into Roman Catholic Church, February.

1926–29   Subeditor, *Times* (London).

1929   *The Man Within.*

1930   *The Name of Action.*

1931   *Rumour at Nightfall.*

1932   *Stamboul Train* (Greene's first "entertainment").

1934   *It's a Battlefield.*

1934   Trip to West Africa (Liberia and Sierra Leone).

1935   *The Basement Room* (stories).

1935   *England Made Me.*

1935–39   Film critic, *The Spectator.*

1936   *Journey Without Maps* (travel book on the African journey).

1936   *A Gun for Sale* (U.S. title: *This Gun For Hire*).

1938   *Brighton Rock.*

1938   Trip to Mexico to report on religious persecution.

1939   *The Lawless Roads* (travel book on the Mexican journey). (U.S. title: *Another Mexico*)

1940   *The Power and the Glory.*

1940–41	Literary editor, *The Spectator*.
1941–44	Attached to British Foreign Office.
1942	*British Dramatists*.
1942	*This Gun for Hire* (alternative title to *A Gun for Sale*) filmed in Hollywood.
1942–43	In Sierra Leone with British Secret Service.
1943	*Ministry of Fear*.
1947	*Nineteen Stories*.
1948	Film scripts by Greene for *Brighton Rock, Fallen Idol* (an adaptation of Greene's story, "The Basement Room").
1948	*The Heart of the Matter*.
1949	Film script of *The Third Man*.
1950	*The Third Man* and *The Fallen Idol* (narrative versions of the film scripts).
1951	*The Lost Childhood and Other Essays*.
1951	*The End of the Affair*.
1951	In Kenya and Malaya as correspondent.
1953	*The Living Room* (play) produced in London. Published same year.
1954	*Twenty-one Stories*.
1954	In Indo-China as correspondent for *New Republic*.
1955	*Loser Take All*.
1955	*The Quiet American*.
1957	*The Potting Shed* (play) produced in London; published same year.
1958	*Our Man in Havana*.
1959	*The Complaisant Lover* (play) produced in London; published same year.
1959	Trip to the Congo.
1960	Film script of *Our Man in Havana*.

1961   *A Burnt-Out Case.*

1961   *In Search of a Character: Two African Journals.*

1963   *In Search of Reality* (stories).

1964   *Carving a Statue* (play) produced in London.

1966   *The Comedians.*

1967   Film script of *The Comedians.*

1967   *May We Borrow Your Husband?* (stories).

1969   *Collected Essays.*

1969   *Travels with My Aunt.*

1971   *A Sort of Life* (autobiography).

Notes on the Editor and Contributors

SAMUEL HYNES. Professor of English, Northwestern University. Author of *The Pattern of Hardy's Poetry* (1961), *The Edwardian Turn of Mind* (1968), *Edwardian Occasions* (1972), and *Twentieth Century Interpretations of 1984*.

W. H. AUDEN. Poet, dramatist, librettist, critic, translator. *The Dyer's Hand* (1963) is a selection of his critical writings. Other critical books are *The Enchafèd Flood* (1950) and *Secondary Worlds* (1968).

JOSEPH IGNATIUS CARTMELL. Catholic theologian and writer. Formerly Professor of Dogmatic Theology at St. Joseph's College, Upholland, England. Reviser of Joseph Faa di Bruno's *Catholic Belief* (London: Burns, 1940) and author of several books.

IAN GREGOR. Professor of English, University of Kent, Canterbury. Co-author of *The Moral and the Story* (with Brian Nichols) [1962], and of *William Golding: a Critical Study* (with Mark Kinkead-Weekes) [1967]. His most recent book is an edition of Matthew Arnold's *Culture and Anarchy* (1971).

RICHARD HOGGART. Assistant Director-General of UNESCO since 1970; Professor of English, Birmingham University, since 1962. His books include *The Uses of Literacy* (1957), *W. H. Auden* (1957), and a two-volume collection of his essays, *Speaking to Each Other* (1970).

FRANK KERMODE. Lord Northcliffe Professor of Modern English Literature at University College, London. Author of *Romantic Image* (1957), *Puzzles and Epiphanies* (1962), and *The Sense of an Ending* (1967).

R. W. B. LEWIS. Professor of English, Yale University. Author of *The American Adam* (1955), *The Picaresque Saint* (1959), and *Trials of the Word* (1965).

FRANÇOIS MAURIAC (1885–1970). French Catholic novelist, essayist and critic. Winner of the Nobel Prize, 1952.

GEORGE ORWELL (1903–50). English novelist and political writer, best known for *Nineteen Eighty-four* (1949) and *Animal Farm* (1945). His critical writings are included in the four-volume *Collected Essays, Journalism and Letters* (1968).

THE REVEREND GENE D. PHILLIPS, S.J. A member of the Loyola University of Chicago English Department, where he teaches literature and film. His book, *Graham Greene Comes to the Screen: The Films of his Fiction,* will be published in late 1972.

SIMON RAVEN. Critic, novelist, dramatist. Author of ten novels. His numerous dramatizations for the B.B.C. include Huxley's *Point Counterpoint* and Trollope's *The Way We Live Now.*

MARTIN SHUTTLEWORTH. Head of Fine Art at Portsmouth Polytechnic. He is a playwright, a novelist, and a translator from the Spanish.

PHILIP STRATFORD. Teaches English at the University of Western Ontario. He is the author of *Faith and Fiction: Creative Process in Greene and Mauriac* (1964).

DEREK TRAVERSI. Formerly an official of the British Council; now Professor of English at Swarthmore College. His many books on Shakespeare include *Approach to Shakespeare* (1938), *Shakespeare: the Roman Plays* (1963), and *Shakespeare: the Last Phase* (1955).

EVELYN WAUGH (1903–66). English novelist and travel writer, and, like Greene, a Roman Catholic convert.

MORTON DAUWEN ZABEL (1901–64). Editor of *Poetry* magazine, and Professor of English at the University of Chicago. A critic of the novel, whose most important book is *Craft and Character in Modern Fiction* (1957).

Selected Bibliography

Editions

The standard edition of Greene's works is the new *Collected Edition* (London: William Heinemann, Limited, 1970–   ). As of January, 1972, seven of the novels have been reprinted in this edition, each with a new introduction by Greene.

The Collected Essays (London: The Bodley Head, 1969) includes most of the essays of *The Lost Childhood* (1951), some rewritten or expanded, plus a number of more recent pieces.

Bibliographies

Brennan, Neil. "Bibliography," in Robert O. Evans, ed., *Graham Greene: Some Critical Considerations*. Lexington: University of Kentucky Press, 1963, pp. 245–76. The most complete primary bibliography. Also includes reviews, critical books, and articles on Greene.

Beebe, Maurice. "Criticism of Graham Greene: A Selected Checklist with an index to Studies of Separate Works," *Modern Fiction Studies* 3 (Autumn, 1957), 281–88. The work-by-work index is especially useful, though it is now somewhat out of date.

Hargreaves, Phylis. "Graham Greene: A Selected Bibliography," *Modern Fiction Studies* 3 (Autumn, 1957), 269–80. A checklist of books and articles by Greene.

Vann, J. Don. *Graham Greene: A Checklist of Criticism*. Kent, Ohio: Kent State University Press, 1970. Includes books and articles about Greene, and a chronological list of important reviews.

Some of the critical books listed below also contain bibliographies, as indicated.

Criticism

Allott, Kenneth and Miriam Farris. *The Art of Graham Greene.* London: Hamish Hamilton, 1951. The first book in English on Greene; deals with the recurrent, "obsessional" ideas in the novels through *The Heart of the Matter.* A short bibliography.

Atkins, John. *Graham Greene,* revised edition. London: Calder & Boyers, 1966. A sprightly study of Greene's works, admiring the fiction but regretting the theology.

Cargas, H. J., ed. *Graham Greene.* St. Louis: Herder, n.d. (1969). Nine essays covering Greene's work through *The Comedians.* In The Christian Critics Series.

De Pange, Victor. *Graham Greene.* Paris: Éditions Universitaires, 1958. A monograph on Greene's themes and techniques, by one of Greene's many French admirers. The bibliography includes other criticism in French.

De Vitis, A. A. *Graham Greene.* New York: Twayne, 1964. Concentrates on the place of religion in Greene's works. Bibliography.

Evans, Robert Owen, ed. *Graham Greene: Some Critical Considerations.* Lexington: University of Kentucky Press, 1963. Fourteen essays by British and American critics that cover Greene's career. Bibliography.

Francis L. Kunkel. *The Labyrinthine Ways of Graham Greene.* New York: Sheed & Ward, 1959. A study of Greene's works, including the travel books and plays, that concentrates on themes and ideas, and particularly on the theological ideas. Sketchy bibliography.

Lodge, David. *Graham Greene.* New York: Columbia University Press, 1966. A 48-page pamphlet, in the Columbia Essays on Modern Writers series, by a critic who is himself a novelist. Selected bibliography.

Madaule, Jacques. *Graham Greene.* Paris: Éditions du Temps Présent, 1949. Themes and techniques in the novels through *The Heart of the Matter.*

Mesnet, Marie-Beatrice. *Graham Greene and the Heart of the Matter.* London: Cresset Press, 1954. An essay on the spiritual themes of Greene's "trilogy": *Brighton Rock, The Power and the Glory,* and *The Heart of the Matter.* Bibliography.

Pryce-Jones, David. *Graham Greene.* Edinburgh: Oliver & Boyd, 1963. A short introduction to Greene's work; in the Writers and Critics series. Bibliography.

Stratford, Philip. *Faith and Fiction: Creative Process in Greene and Mauriac.* Notre Dame, Indiana: University of Notre Dame Press, 1964. A study of two Catholic novelists, and the influence of their Catholicism on their writing. Bibliographical notes.